PLAYING IN THE BOX

PLAYING
IN
THE BOX

A PRACTICAL GUIDE FOR HELPING ATHLETES DEVELOP THEIR MENTAL GAME

DR. PETE TEMPLE

LIONCREST

PUBLISHING

PLAYING IN THE BOX

A Practical Guide for Helping Athletes Develop Their Mental Game

ISBN   978-1-5445-0188-8 *Hardcover*

978-1-5445-1279-2 *Paperback*

978-1-5445-1278-5 *Ebook*

My parents, Dick and Nancy, for putting a
loving foundation under my feet.

My sister, Patti, for leading the way and being my pathfinder.

My children, Mady and Pace, for inspiring me and making life fun.

My wife and best friend, Paige, for believing
in me and making life beautiful.

This book would not exist if not for you.

Acknowledgments:

My coaches, who gave me a passion for sports.

My teammates, who shared that passion with me.

My athletes, who keep that passion alive.

Philippians 4:13

CONTENTS

INTRODUCTION

. . . . .

THE UNBALANCED ATHLETE

When I played Little League back in the late seventies, we rode our bikes to practice, or our parents dropped us off at the town baseball field. A few parents would hang around and watch, but most either left to go to work or run errands.

Our coach was usually a young guy who'd played baseball in high school, and he had all the expertise we needed. Most of us knew how to catch and hit, and the coach would show us how to backhand a grounder or pivot at second base for a double play. He would hit grounders for the infielders and fly balls for the outfielders, and that was practice. We played twelve to fifteen games a year, and our seasons ended in early August, so families could take vacations. When fall came, we played football.

Thirty years later, my son started Little League. And I quickly realized things had changed.

I was one of five coaches for my son's team. None of the players rode their bikes to practice because they had too much to carry, such as bats and equipment bags with their names stitched onTO them. The dads built a custom batting cage so the coaches could give regular hitting instruction. In addition, some kids had private hitting coaches and pitching coaches.

My son's team had a fifty-game schedule. Half of those games were out of town, and some of them were out of state. Many of the parents would stay to watch practice, and the games were huge events. Families brought lawn chairs, canopies, and coolers, settling in for three hours of watching twelve-year-olds play baseball.

Not only was this atmosphere more intense than any I'd experienced as a Little Leaguer, but the kids themselves were different. They were fitter and stronger than my teammates and I had been. The kids on my son's team "hydrated" with Gatorade and ate protein bars. Their physical and technical skills were way beyond those of the twelve-year-olds of my day. Many of them had been to baseball camps, and some played year-round or for more than one team. The players' and parents' commitment to the sport was far more significant than it had been in my day.

During the last thirty years, other youth sports have changed in the same way. Many young swimmers train twice a day, putting in ten-thousand-meter workouts and pulling on expensive, high-tech racing suits for big meets. Young basketball players are playing year-round on travel or AAU teams, developing blinding on-court speed, and ankle-snapping crossover dribbles that make college coaches drool.

Whatever the sport, today's young athletes' focus on their physical and technical development has elevated the quality of their overall play. But it's also elevated the expectations these athletes face. And that increased pressure has exposed a gaping hole in these athletes' training: their mental preparation.

We can train high school athletes to throw a vicious slider or run a mile in under five minutes, but we don't do enough to help them cope with the mental and emotional aspects of competing at a high level under the pressure of all their elite coaching and training. The result is that a lot of young athletes, despite their incredible skills and fitness, struggle to excel at and enjoy the sports for which they train so hard.

THREE GEARS WORKING TOGETHER

When I talk about the "complete athlete," I am referring to someone who has the highly developed physical, technical, and mental tools they need to succeed. Every successful athlete has those three gears—the physical, technical, and mental—and those three gears turn simultaneously. Each gear helps the other two turn more smoothly, and when each gear is contributing, the athletic process seems almost effortless. Think OF Steph Curry darting down an open lane to drop in a floater over his defender. He makes it look so easy.

However, if one of those gears stalls, the other two also get stuck.

Complete Athlete

Physical

Technical

Mental

As a sports psychologist, I've worked with dozens of young players who have excellent technical and physical skills they've spent years developing. Their parents have also made significant investments of time, money, and emotional support. During practice, these young athletes can fly around the court or casually line one curveball after another to the gap in center. But during games, something happens. They become tentative. They miss shots they never miss in practice. They get angry and lose confidence. They're unsure how to react in situations they've dealt with hundreds of times during training.

These athletes come to me in frustration. Boys and girls. They've spent so much time training and practicing that their expectations of themselves and the expectations of their parents, coaches, and teammates combine to put tremendous pressure on them.

I try to help these athletes find a better balance between their three gears. Most of the time, it's the mental gear that's slowing them down, and I help them understand the fundamental components of that mental gear, and how they can strengthen those components. Our goal is to build strong mental mechanics—the thought processes and habits that keep their mental gear sound and reliable. When these athletes can develop their mental game in this way, their cognitive, physical, and technical gears can turn in unison again.

This book will help you develop your mental gear. You'll learn techniques for handling pressure, controlling your emotions, moving past your mistakes, and building a frame of mind that allows you to excel at and love your sport again. A well-developed mental gear allows you to deploy your technical and physical abilities at the highest level. In addition to preparing you to compete, a finely tuned mental gear helps you overcome the inevitable challenges and setbacks that are part of sports. You want your mental gear to be just as fit, fast, and graceful as your other two gears.

If you become an Olympian or qualify for the PGA Tour, there are all kinds of mental-skill coaches available to you. That's great. But why should you wait until you've already "made it" to address your mental gear? Wouldn't you prefer to start developing some of the mental skills at an earlier age, when it could do you a lot of good?

THE IMPORTANCE OF MENTAL TRAINING

I enjoy having athletes as clients. They are disciplined and motivated, and when we work on their mental game, they often see quick results. However, it wasn't until my own kids started playing sports—and I could see just how advanced the physical and technical training had become—that I realized that society isn't being systematic about the way we're working with young athletes.

We give them terrific tools for learning technical skills and increasing their physical abilities, but we do nothing about the mental aspects of sports. We just let them figure those out on their own. For that reason, I hope coaches and parents will also read this book and understand that our young athletes need more than training and coaching to succeed.

Yogi Berra was once quoted saying, "Baseball is 90 percent mental. The other half is physical." While Yogi's math was faulty, his perceptions weren't: in sports, mental preparation is paramount. Coaches and parents talk about it all the time, but most don't fully understand it or know how to teach it. There is also a stigma around it. If your kid can't hit a curveball, you have no qualms about hiring a hitting coach to help them. But if your kid doesn't do well in high-pressure situations, it's a sign of weakness. This simply isn't the case. The athletes I work with don't have personality flaws or suffer from psychological instability; they come to see me so they can become better, just as they go to the batting cages so their coach can fine-tune their swing.

Every athlete is different. Some players are easygoing and roll with the punches, while others are intense and blow up when they fail. I've worked with many athletes who have said at the outset of our work together, "Dr. Pete, I know I freak out when something doesn't go right on the court, but that's just the way I am." I usually tell them, "Well, that's the way you are now, but we can work at that so it's not the way you continue to be."

OUT OF SYNC

Pretend for a moment you're a basketball player. Every day you practice your jump shot from the corner beyond the three-point line. An assistant coach works with you, throwing every type of pass imaginable—a perfect bounce pass one time or a hard line drive the next. It doesn't matter. You catch, square up, elevate, and release, catch, square up, elevate, and release. Every day you work on getting two hands on the ball, squaring up to the hoop, elevating, and releasing the ball. Catch, square, elevate, release. You practice over and over until the motion is as natural as brushing your teeth. Catch, square, elevate, release. The balls drop through the net like they're being sucked in by a vacuum. Over and over. Your coach is yelling things at you and other players are boiling around you working on their own routines, but none of that bothers you because your job is to catch, square, elevate, and release. Your arms get stronger, your motion gets smoother, and your thoughts, well, they kind of disappear.

There you are. All three gears are spinning in concert.

But when it's game time, distracting thoughts enter your

mind. You think, *I hope I don't screw up* or *What if my shot is off?* You think about that some more. You're in the lineup because you are one of the best shooters on the team. But what if you miss a few? Will your teammates no longer pass it to you? Will the coach pull you from the game? When the game starts, your shot feels awkward. You hesitate to shoot and instead start looking for someone cutting to the hoop so you can get rid of the ball. Your play slows down. The shots won't fall and your passes to cutting teammates arrive too late. You react to these events with frustration rather than getting back on defense like you're supposed to. You're feeling lost and miserable.

This is your mental gear hindering your physical and technical gears.

One year, the NHL draft was in Chicago, and I was invited to talk to a group of players who were hoping to realize their dream of playing professionally. When you speak to any group of athletes and ask them if they think the mental aspect of their game is important, everyone nods in agreement. I've never had a coach or athlete say the mental game is not essential; in fact, they often say having the right mental approach is the most important thing. These hockey players were the same way. They all agreed they needed to have a strong mental game as well as superior physical and technical skills.

I asked these players, "If I told you to work for an hour on your physical skills, could you come back and tell me what you did?" They all said they could. They'd work on their skating speed and endurance, or they'd hit the weight room to build their upper-body strength. "What if I told you to work on your technical skills for an hour?" I said. "Could you come back and tell me what you had done?" They said they could. They'd work on their stick handling or their skating. "What if I told you to work on your mental game?" I said. "Could you come back and tell me what you had done?" The players just sat and stared at me. They couldn't tell me what they would do. They had no idea.

The hockey players, like most athletes, understood that their mental state—their mental game—affects their performance. They knew it was just as important as—if not more important than—how fast they skated or how they passed the puck. But they didn't know the fundamentals of that mental game—what the key components of it are, and how to practice and improve those components.

Athletes develop their technical and physical gears by understanding the fundamentals of each of those gears. If you want to score runs in baseball, you have to know how to hit. If you want to stop the other team from scoring, you have to know how to field. Once you know what the fundamentals are (hitting and fielding), you can practice and master the mechanics and turn those fundamentals into finely tuned skills. This is why your hitting coach breaks down each element of hitting and gives you drills to practice those elements. You work on your stance in the batter's box. You work on torquing your hips for more power. The same is true for your physical gear. Hitters work on their strength and flexibility. They do drills to improve their bat speed and their reaction times.

You develop the mental game the same way. Athletes have to understand the fundamentals—manage your confidence, direct and control your thinking, regulate your emotions, handle mistakes and bad breaks, and maximize your training. These fundamentals of the mental game are turned into skills by developing mental mechanics that can be practiced and mastered.

And as this group of amateur hockey players demonstrated, most young athletes today don't know the fundamentals of their mental gear, let alone the mechanics for improving and mastering those fundamentals. Through coaching, equipment, and training, we're helping them develop their physical and technical gears but offering no help with their mental gear. These athletes know their mental gear is crucial, and they talk about it all the time. But they have no idea how to develop it, and neither do their coaches. As a result, athletes and coaches alike tend to overemphasize the physical and the technical gears to compensate for a weak mental gear.

This widespread failure to help young athletes hone their mental gear is cheating athletes by depriving them of what they need and want. It's not enough to tell a player to "hang tough" after striking out. Our athletes deserve better than that.

MENTAL MECHANICS

You build up the strength of your mental gear the same way you develop physical and technical skills. Just as you work out to improve your fitness or do drills to perfect your backswing, you can strengthen your mental gear by practicing proper mechanics.

The mechanics of the mental gear are based on cognitive psychology—the study of mental processes that affect our behavior. The discipline uses the following frame: an event occurs, we consider it, and then we react or respond to it. Cognitive psychologists focus on the moment in the middle—the one before we act—and seek to explain how our thinking influences our responses.

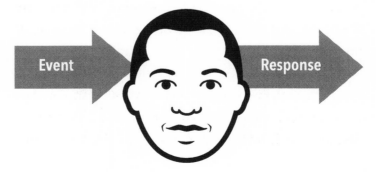

Sports psychologists use cognitive psychology techniques to improve performance. In sports, events happen all the time that prompt athletes to react in some way. Some events, such as scoring a touchdown, are good, while others, such as missing an open jump shot from the corner, are bad. Although good events can trigger a celebration that distracts athletes, most often it's adverse events that cause our mental gear to wobble.

Pretend again you're the basketball player we described earlier, our catch-and-shoot, Kyle-Korver-like three-point specialist. It's game time and you are tight and nervous. You've missed your first corner three and you think, *I don't have the right rhythm tonight.* When you think that way, chances are you will continue to struggle with your shot. Instead, what if you thought back to your practice sessions? *Catch, square, elevate, release.* It comes back to you now, that feeling. *Catch, square, elevate, release.* That cadence gets locked in your head, and all the other thoughts get pushed out. *Catch, square, elevate, release.* And that's what you do when the pass comes to you in the corner. It's quiet in your head, the hoop looks huge from the height of your jump, and your release is as sweet as it is in practice. Swish.

I call this "dealing with the dis-es." You don't want to be dis-ed, meaning disappointed, distracted, or discouraged. It's natural to feel disappointed when you miss. But if that disappointment affects what happens next, that's a sign of a wobbly mental gear. Your shot is a technical skill, and you've worked hard to perfect it. Your jumping height is a physical skill that you've also developed. Analyzing a miss and putting it past you so you can be ready for the next shot is a mental skill that you can also develop. *Catch, square, elevate, release.* Training our thinking in this way is the foundation of sports psychology.

Here's the point: the way we think affects our performance. If you're not aware of that, you'll beat yourself up after a bad play and wonder why your confidence is in the tank. Your confidence will erode because you'll chip away at it. As you become more aware of how you think—and avoid the thinking that undermines your confidence— you'll enjoy your sport more and have greater success at it. Just remind yourself, *It's just a miss. It happens.* Then take a deep breath and be ready to hit the next one.

IT'S TIME TO TRAIN YOUR BRAIN

I recently did a workshop for a team where I demonstrated how the brain controls the body. I tied a small metal washer to a string and held it up by the end of the string for the players to see. My arm, hand, and fingers were still and so was the washer. But then I said out loud what I had started to think. "Circle, circle, circle," I said in simple and direct language while thinking the same thought. My arm, hand, and fingers remained still, but the washer did what I told it to do: it made a small, slow circle.

Then I began thinking something else and voiced the thought out loud. "This is a stupid idea," I said. "These guys are probably laughing at me. I never should have done this!" As I said this, the washer quickly slowed and eventually stopped.

This might seem like a clever parlor trick, but it isn't. I explained to the team that the body is programmed by millions of years of evolution to follow the brain and to do what the brain says. When I was saying "circle, circle, circle," the nerve endings in my fingers were twitching and tugging and doing whatever they could to follow the strong and direct command my brain was sending. When I began to jam that positive communication with judgment, worry, and doubt, the body's performance was thrown off track. My mental gear was jammed, and that caused my physical gear to shut down. The washer stopped moving.

This demonstration helps explain why the brain is your most essential muscle. It's the one your body always follows, and it's always at work. If you're serious about your sport, you're always thinking, whether you're on the court or on the bench. This is why you need to look at the brain as something you can train.

This book can help you do that. *Playing in the BOX* is for anyone who understands that the mental game is important, but doesn't know how to train for it. This book contains techniques that will help you improve the functioning of your mental gear. It will help you understand your mental fundamentals and teach you the mental mechanics that allow you to manage and improve those fundamentals—the same way you go out to the driveway and work on your free throws or go to a park to improve your soccer foot skills.

When athletes are struggling or not seeing the results they want, they typically double down on their training. They spend more hours at the gym or stay after practice. Hard work is always a good idea, but often these athletes are targeting the wrong gear. Focusing on the wrong gear can compound the athlete's frustration—"I know I work harder in practice than anyone. I just don't get it!"—and lead to discouragement and a loss of confidence. How do you know when the mental gear needs the extra time? Consider these questions:

1. Do you consistently perform better in practice than in games or competitions?
2. Do you feel your game isn't improving despite the hard work you put into it?
3. Is your confidence low or inconsistent?

4. Do you struggle to bounce back from a bad play or a bad game?
5. Is it becoming harder for you to get motivated?
6. Are you overly concerned about playing poorly or "choking"?
7. Are you enjoying your sport less than you used to?

If you find yourself answering yes to some of these questions, keeping reading. Like most athletes, you probably need help training your mental gear. Adding mental training might help you more than spending extra time in the weight room or gym.

I also hope this book will enhance your experience as an athlete. I work with a lot of athletes who have a love-hate relationship with their sport. They practice and train so much that when they don't play well, they feel profoundly disappointed and discouraged. If you've had this experience, know that this book can help you navigate those ups and downs in the future. While ups and downs are a natural part of sports, a strong mental game will help you relax and enjoy the ride.

Are you ready to learn how?

CHAPTER 1

· · · · ·

THE COMPLETE ATHLETE

I knew fairly early in junior that guys were going to be better than I was. I had to find a different area where I could push myself to the next level, and that was the mental game.

—BRADEN HOLTBY, VEZINA TROPHY
WINNER, STANLEY CUP CHAMPION

When athletes consistently perform well over an extended period of time, such as when a baseball player has a twenty-game hitting streak or a golfer is routinely shooting under par, they often say things like "I was just in the zone" or "I wasn't overthinking anything. I was just playing." When you hear this, it's a sign that the athlete's three gears are all well-trained and moving in unison. When an athlete's physical, technical, and mental gears are moving together smoothly, they can achieve the peak performance all athletes strive for.

Unfortunately, many athletes never develop that mental gear. They commit the time and energy needed to get bigger, stronger, and faster, and they work on their technical skills in the pool, on the court, or on the field. But they usually ignore the most important muscle—the brain. This creates an imbalance.

Unbalanced vs. Balanced Athlete

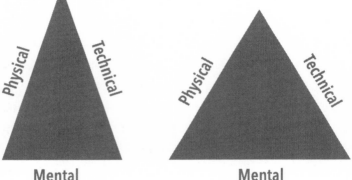

Here's another way to look at it. The tall triangle on the left depicts an athlete who has well-developed physical and technical gears but an underdeveloped mental gear. This results in a weak foundation. This triangle looks flimsy, like even a breeze could topple it over. That's an unbalanced athlete.

But the triangle on the right is better proportioned. The mental gear is as well developed as the physical and technical gears, creating a stout foundation and a stronger center of gravity. Not even a stiff wind will knock that structure over. It's balanced and stable and difficult to push around.

BACK IN TIME

If you compare a high school athlete today to one from the seventies or eighties, today's player would look far different physically than my teammates or I did thirty years ago. We trained our physical gear by doing push-ups, sit-ups, and chin-ups. Today's athlete builds his abs and obliques under the direction of trainers in state-of-the-art facilities filled with incline treadmills, Cybex machines, and racks of dumbbells. We chugged RC Cola and gobbled Baby Ruth bars for energy on a hot day. They "hydrate" with Gatorade and "replenish" with PowerBars. Our moms took snapshots of us at the plate using an Instamatic. Their at-bats are recorded on high-definition video so they can watch later and refine their swing. Today's athlete is a different person altogether, better trained physically and technically than we ever dreamed was possible.

Yet, somehow, their mental game looks just like ours. When we struck out, we kicked the dirt in frustration and stomped back to the dugout to sulk. So do they. Why has that aspect of sports not changed?

Everyone knows an athlete has to be stronger, faster, and better than their opponents if they want to be competitive. We know that their sport-specific skills and fundamentals have to be honed to perfection with practice and training if they want a winning season. We also know that psychology and mental preparedness can make a difference in an athlete's performance. Players and coaches always talk about the value of mental toughness. Ty Cobb, who set ninety Major League Baseball records during his career, once said, "The most important part of a player's body is above his shoulders." Basketball coach Bobby Knight similarly told his basketball players, "Mental toughness is to physical as four is to one."

If mental preparation is so important, why don't athletes do more about it?

Athletes typically won't learn how to develop their mental gear until they achieve elite status and their coaches introduce them to the tools they need to do it. Athletes might receive this kind of psychological training if they're good enough to earn a college scholarship or when they turn pro. Organizations have made an investment in these athletes, and coaches understand that to get the most from an athlete, the athlete's mental gear has to be as strong and smooth-flowing as the technical and physical gears.

Most of you will never be professional athletes, but that

doesn't mean you can't be complete athletes. You can pump up your mental muscle just like you pump up your physical ones. It takes time and practice, but once the mental gear is turning as fast as the other two, your game will improve, become more consistent, and feel like fun again.

PLAY SMART

Having a strong mental gear can carry you through when your other gears fail. Have you ever heard an athlete say, "I knew I wasn't feeling 100 percent, so I had to play smarter" or "I knew from the first inning that I didn't have my best stuff, so I had to find another way to win"? Being "smarter" and using "another way to win" involves the mental game.

The mental gear is critical in all sports. I once worked with a cross-country runner who complained about "hitting the wall" in her races. During races, cross-country runners are typically running at the very top level of their physical abilities. Their heart rates are at their maximum levels, and they have to maintain this even as they negotiate uneven terrain and keep their eyes on their competitors. It's stressful. The runner I was working with explained that when she started thinking about how hard it was, her legs would get heavy, she'd struggle to breathe, and she'd tighten up. When this happened, she would slow down, sometimes running slower in races than she did on training runs.

Once she and I established that the "wall" was predictable and a product of her doubts, she was able to work toward correcting the situation. She and I developed some mental games and practiced them so that she could respond to those moments that used to tank her performance.

For example, she used affirmations between races to overcome the negative thoughts she had during races. She had a note on her mirror that said, "I attack hills." Every time she brushed her teeth, she said, "I attack hills. I attack hills." She developed a pre-race routine where she visualized running up to a hill and attacking it. Now, instead of trudging up a hill and letting doubts unravel her confidence, she uses a cadence of "go, go, go, go" to get those thoughts out of her head. She got the upper hand. Now, she is the one attacking the hill instead of the other way around.

Since she had practiced with affirmations and visualizations and had polished and lubricated her mental gear, her physical gear reacted. She trained on hills and perfected an efficient technique for running up them. Then, with those two gears and her mental gear turning in unison, "the wall" never appeared and she continued powering to the top. The key here is that she practiced and worked that mental gear with the same diligence that she did her training runs.

IN THE BOX

The first step in developing a stronger mental game is recognizing what it feels like to be in the zone—or what I call "the BOX." Once you know that feeling, you can train your mental focus so it's easy to get back into the BOX when something throws you out.

In 1908, psychologists Robert Yearks and John Dodson looked at the relationship among performance, thinking, and emotion. They wanted to know how our thoughts affect our emotions and then, in turn, our performance. Their results gave us a specific tool that we can apply to athletics.

Yerkes and Dodson found that a person's performance improves with mental arousal but declines when the person becomes too aroused. The results of the Yearks-Dodson study were a perfect bell curve. On one end was low performance—what athletes refer to as being "flat" emotionally. There's no excitement or nervousness. It's how you might feel when you're going against an inferior opponent.

On the other end of the curve, you are in your head too

much. Too many thoughts are swirling in your mind. Instead of being emotionally flat, you're freaked out, anxious, and tense.

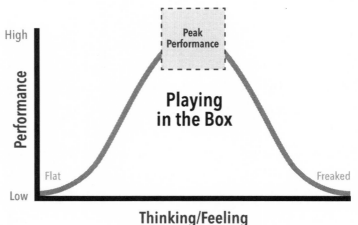

Whether flat or freaked, your performance will suffer. You're either unengaged and sluggish, or you're trying to remember everything at once, and worrying about screwing up and losing the game.

However, there is a third option. I call it the BOX. The BOX sits at the top of the bell curve and represents the ideal competitive mindset. This is the place where your thoughts and emotions lead to optimal performance. This is where you always want to be. It's your happy place when you're there and your destination when you're not.

Being in the BOX feels different for every athlete. Some

have a calm, quiet mind, while others have a sensation of energy or excitement. Once you figure out what the BOX feels like for you, you can use your thoughts and routines to consistently get you there.

Your thoughts are crucial to staying in the BOX because emotions will follow your thoughts. Thinking brings the feeling. When your thinking is off, you won't feel right and you won't be in the BOX.

It's essential for athletes to recognize when they are no longer in the BOX and to develop the tools they need to get back in. This can often be a simple adjustment to your thinking. A good example is a hitter who was just fooled by a slider. The pitch was heading toward the strike zone but sailed outside just as the batter swung at it, causing him to miss badly. That kind of play can knock a player out of the BOX by staying in his mind for several more pitches. On the other hand, a player skilled in mental mechanics can recognize that they have left the BOX and will consciously refocus their thoughts on the next pitch, forgetting about that nasty slider.

There are also a couple of ways athletes can picture the BOX. In the example above, the player imagined that he'd been knocked out of the BOX and took steps to get back in. Other players picture the BOX as their peak performance zone that can sometimes get crowded with unwanted and distracting thoughts. In that case, their mental adjustments involve clearing out the BOX so they can get back to focusing on the next play. As you develop your own mental mechanics, you'll find an image that works for you.

LEARNING THE FUNDAMENTALS

Regardless of what sport you play, each of the three gears—the technical, physical, and mental—has fundamental elements.

The technical gear for basketball, for instance, comprises such sport-specific elements as dribbling, shooting, rebounding, and so on. The physical gear comprises fundamental aspects of fitness, including strength, agility, explosiveness, and quickness. A well-developed mental gear also requires a mastery of fundamentals—*mental fundamentals*. These fundamentals are as important to an athlete's success as a fluid swing or a graceful throwing motion.

The first mental fundamental is the ability to manage your **confidence**. The second is **mindset,** which is the capacity to direct your thinking in a way that helps you and doesn't impede your performance. A third mental fundamental is the power to regulate your **emotion** so that when you feel anger, frustration, anxiety, or elation it doesn't distract you and take you out of the game. A fourth fundamental, **resilience**, is knowing how to handle disruptions. In sports, disruptive events happen all the time, and the best athletes are those who know how to cope with them quickly and efficiently so that they instantly become insignificant.

The fifth fundamental of the mental gear is a little different from the first four because it is directly related to the work you do on the physical and technical ones. I call it **drive**, or "maximizing training," and it means that when you work out or practice, you do it intentionally with a sense of purpose and a focus on specific goals.

MENTAL MECHANICS AND THE BOX

Mastering the mental mechanics—the thought processes and habits that help you fine-tune your confidence, mindset, emotional control, resilience, and drive and turn those fundamentals into skills—requires the same diligence with which you train your muscles or practice your skills. With practice, you can gain proficiency over the mechanics and add a critical new dimension to your game. These psychological skills are a largely untapped resource for most athletes, but once you open up that reservoir, the possibility for improvement and newfound pleasure and satisfaction are boundless. What's more, your dexterity with the mental mechanics are transferable to other aspects of your life and can pay off in other endeavors long after you leave the playing field.

Once you gain some mastery over the mental mechanics, you can use them to keep yourself in the BOX or help you return to it. For example, if you check in with yourself before a game against an inferior opponent and discover you feel flat, you can tweak your routine to energize yourself for the climb back into the BOX. If you're freaked—the way you get when you're playing a team that has a winning streak against you—you can leverage a routine that will mellow you out a little. If music is part of your routine (as it is for many athletes) you can keep three playlists—one for when you are just where you want to be, one for when you need a boost, and one that calms your anxieties.

Finding the BOX can be as simple as learning what works for you. For example, before a competition, you might prefer to go off by yourself, put some music on, and start visualizing the competition. If that approach unleashes an adrenaline rush and causes anxiety, you might try relaxing with teammates instead. You may try several things before you find one that works for you, and that's okay. Keep searching for an effective strategy until you discover one. It's vital that you know what you can do to get back into the BOX, and it's critical that you practice that technique and use it routinely. Once you have an

approach that works, it's like having a go-to pitch or r
that you can always count on.

When your mental mechanics are on point, peak performance will follow. You start strong, and all of your gears
turn freely, working in harmony. Distractions will inev-
itably occur, however. In a split second, you might start
thinking about what happened in the last game or how
hard the next hole is going to be. You'll start stuffing the
BOX full of the past and the future, as well as all of the
"dis-es"—feelings of being disappointed, distracted, or
discouraged. None of that belongs in the BOX.

You have to protect the BOX by finding the resilience
to empty it of everything except you and the present
moment. Then you are right back into it. Athletes have
to know when they are in the BOX, how to get back in,
and how to keep everything out that doesn't belong.

As you learn how to get in and stay in the BOX, you'll
come to understand the importance of confidence, mindset, emotion, resilience, and drive. These are all elements
of the mental toolbox that this book will help you build
and use. With that in mind, let's move on to the first and
most important tool—confidence.

CHAPTER 2

. . . . .

CONFIDENCE

If you don't believe in yourself, no one else will.

—SHERYL SWOOPES

Confidence is the most important single factor in this game, and no matter how great your natural talent, there is only one way to obtain and sustain it: work.

—JACK NICKLAUS

Several years ago, I met Luke, a gifted multisport athlete who had been moved up to play on the varsity basketball team after his freshman year. I met him in the summer between his freshman and sophomore years. During those summer practices, Luke was a standout player. He flew all over the court, playing tight defense, launching jump shots, and driving to the rim. He seemed to have an instinct for the game; he was always in the right place at the right time, and the coach trusted him to make good decisions with the ball. Although Luke was a humble kid, he admitted to me that in practice, he felt like one of the best players on the team.

During his first few summer league games, when fans would come out to fill the gym, Luke felt like a completely different player. He was nervous and tentative. He passed up open shots and forced passes to teammates who weren't ready for them. In games, he felt like the new kid, and he tried to fit in by deferring to his more experienced teammates. He was reluctant to drive when the lane was open. He lost his aggressiveness on the boards, worrying about stealing a rebound from one of his teammates.

Luke's problems were of his own making. His coach was supportive and encouraging. He wasn't the kind of coach who yanked players out of a game or berated them for missing a shot. Despite this reassuring environment, Luke would freeze in games, and this made him frustrated and discouraged. By the time we met, Luke was starting to think the coach made a mistake by bringing him up to varsity.

Luke did not have serious flaws in his physical or technical mechanics. He could jump and run as well as or better than other players, and his shooting, ballhandling, and passing skills were sound from years of playing AAU and club basketball.

Luke's problem was rooted in his mental mechanics. He didn't step on the court and forget how to shoot the basketball; it just felt that way. His mental gear was jamming and getting in the way of what Luke knew how to do so well. In games, he would worry about making mistakes, overthink his actions, and hold the ball too long or get rid of it too quickly. "I'm at the point where I just want to get rid of the ball," Luke told me. "I just want to give it to somebody so I don't mess up. I figure, 'I'll just focus on defense.'"

Despite being one of the best players on the team while practicing, Luke was holding back during games and trying to avoid doing the very things that led to him being put on varsity. He'd lost his confidence.

Confidence is the foundational mental mechanic. It is the key to getting into the BOX. Confidence enhances your mindset, emotional control, resilience, and drive, and when your confidence wanes, these other fundamental elements of the mental gear also grow weaker. Without confidence, players struggle to fully use their physical and technical tools, and their performance suffers. And, as Luke's story shows us, the athlete suffers as well.

Confidence is a basic belief that you are up to the task, whatever that task may be. For some athletes, confidence comes easily and has outsized proportions. They think,

I'm going to play great today! I will dominate! They are supremely confident, which is great as long as the feeling doesn't morph into an arrogance that makes them overbearing and difficult to coach or to play with.

For most athletes, though, confidence is a simple belief that they are ready to succeed at the job before them. This confidence that you will perform well frees you to enter the BOX and get your job done.

However, if you lack confidence and worry that you will play poorly or embarrass yourself, it's impossible to find the BOX and play to your full potential. Athletes who struggle with confidence are accustomed to starting the game outside the BOX. They hope the game goes well so they can start feeling better and find their way into the BOX. They are searching for their confidence and their tentative, uncertain play is the result of that struggle.

THINK IT, FEEL IT, ACHIEVE IT

Coaches and athletes like to talk about how they're feeling. Before the game, the coach walks through the locker room asking his players "How you feeling?" or "You feeling good?" The players are all feeling good. "I feel good," the center says, bumping fists with his coach. "I'm *feeling* it."

This all sounds great, but it's actually backwards.

The main driver of performance is thinking. You must *think* something before you can *feel* it. Picture it as the following equation: confident thinking + confident behavior = confident feeling. Feeling comes from what we think. This is a powerful mechanic because it suggests that by thinking differently, which is entirely in your power, you can change the way you feel. And how you feel directly affects your performance. Here's what that might look like for a golfer:

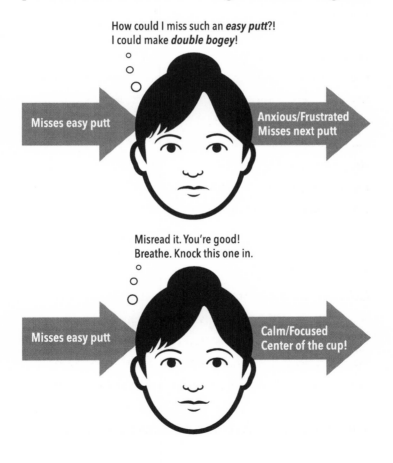

When you choose thoughts that confirm that you are ready and prepared to do what you know how to do, you are more likely to get the result that you want. For athletes, that means getting into the BOX, where you are confident, relaxed, and ready. Thinking confidently or acting confidently doesn't mean you'll hit a walk-off home run in the bottom of the ninth, but it does mean you've put yourself in the best position possible to capitalize on the skills and physical strength you've worked so hard to acquire.

Consider what the opposite scenario is like. How do you feel when your thoughts are *Jeez, I hope I don't screw up*, or *The last time we played this team, they killed us. I'm afraid I'm not going to play well*, or *The game is tight! I hope I don't cost us the game.* It's impossible to be confident when you have thoughts like these. These negative thoughts chip away at your confidence and make it impossible to get into the BOX.

Confidence is created by how you think, but also by your actions. Your brain interprets behavior in ways that will ultimately either help you or hurt you.

I worked for a time with a young quarterback. If he was playing well, he would stand on the sidelines when the other team had the ball, cheering on the defense and rallying the troops for the next series of downs on offense.

He appeared to be upbeat and held himself like someone with supreme confidence and faith in his team's abilities.

However, when the quarterback played poorly, he was likely to stand away from the rest of the team, hanging his head, alone in his own thoughts. He looked defeated and distressed, and he carried himself like someone who was downhearted and lost.

That kind of behavior and posture sent a signal to his brain: "Uh-oh, something is wrong." When your brain gets a signal like that, it tries to figure out what the problem is. This can lead to overanalyzing or traveling back in time to other occasions when you faced defeat or disappointment. The thoughts start to pile up, and before you know it, you have been pushed out of the BOX. It's a chain reaction that starts with hanging your head, slumping your shoulders, or slamming your helmet on the ground.

What we do and how we do it sends a message to the brain. If you get pulled out of a game, you can have a moment to be frustrated, but you can't sit at the end of the bench with your head down. Not only is it a poor visual for the rest of the team, but your own brain reads your behavior as a bigger crisis than it actually is. The BOX is overrun with searching questions and doubts, and your emotions follow those thoughts. How will this impact your performance when the coach wants to put you back in?

MOVING BEYOND FEAR

Young athletes who lack confidence are often apprehensive or fearful. They worry about outcomes and dread making mistakes. They're afraid of embarrassing themselves in front of teammates or spectators. They're rattled and unable to play with all their technical and physical abilities.

If you're in a situation like this, it's not enough to simply tell yourself to "be confident." Instead, remind yourself of all the hard work and practice you've endured to reach this point. Practice thoughts such as, *I can do this. I've worked hard. I'm ready!* Confidence comes from knowing that you've earned the right to be confident. You've done the workouts. You've taken the extra grounders, run the after-practice routes. You've worked long and hard, and it pays to remind yourself of that. Even if you start slow, the effect of thinking this way will compound.

Confidence not only helps you play to your abilities, it often can help you exceed your expectations and the expectations of others. Confidence can make up for things you lack or things others believe you lack. Consider quarterback Peyton Manning. After neck surgery late in his career reduced the velocity of his passes, Manning continued to play in the NFL and even went on to win Super Bowl 50 with the Denver Broncos. Despite being slower and weaker than he had been earlier in his career with Indianapolis, Peyton remained confident as a quarterback by meticulously studying his opponents and finding ways to exploit their weaknesses. He couldn't rifle the ball the way he once could, but that didn't seem to matter.

Another example is former NFL quarterback Kurt Warner, often considered the best undrafted NFL player of all time. Warner played college football at Northern Iowa but didn't start until he was a senior. He wasn't drafted by any NFL teams, found himself playing in the Arena Football League, and was working in a grocery store for $5.50 an hour before getting a chance to play for the St. Louis Rams as their third-string quarterback. When injuries and free agency moves gave Warner a chance to start in 1999, he made the most of his opportunity, throwing three touchdown passes in each of his first three starts—the first NFL quarterback in history to accomplish that feat.

Over the next twelve years, Warner started for three different NFL teams and took two of them to the Super Bowl. In 2017, he was inducted into the Pro Football Hall of Fame.

For people like Warner, confidence is like a Swiss Army knife—it can fix a lot of things. Your opponent may be bigger and more skilled, but if you believe you and your teammates can beat anyone, you can conquer a favored team. Confidence is the common denominator in under-dog upsets, such as when tiny Chaminade defeated the top-ranked University of Virginia in 1982. We see upsets like this in the NCAA March Madness basketball tournament when lower-seeded teams beat far higher-seeded ones. It happens almost every year, and if you closely examine those games, you'll find that the overmatched team was brimming with confidence.

I once attended a football game where the home team lost their quarterback to an injury and then lost their backup quarterback to an injury as well. A running back had to come in and play quarterback, even though the position was unfamiliar to him. He was a confident kid, and he played like he'd been a quarterback his whole life. He convinced himself he was capable of the job, and he was. His team won.

Like a handy Swiss Army knife you always want to keep in your pocket, keep your confidence within reach. Let it be there when you need it. Don't let it come and go. Confidence shouldn't be a reward that comes when you play well and vanishes when you play poorly. Keep it close. Keep it at hand.

There is a robust quality to the confidence of good athletes. Steph Curry and Kobe Bryant are both great shooters, but even they can get cold once in a while. Curry missed ten shots in a row during a playoff game, but he never stopped thinking of himself as a great shooter and ultimately hit the game-winning three-pointer against the Cavaliers. Athletes like Curry and Bryant, even when they are struggling, manage their confidence and are able to ensure that a periodic slump is not going to let them lose confidence. They're still up to the task. They're always ready.

MASTER THE CONFIDENCE EQUATION

You can't control a feeling. You can't grab fear and throw it in the fire. However, when you realize that sadness comes from what you're thinking and what you're doing, then you've got some traction.

Once you understand how the Confidence Equation works (remember: confident thinking + confident behavior = confident feeling), you can control it. When you are aware of what you're thinking and intentionally direct your thinking and behavior, you can get the feeling you desire.

CONFIDENT THINKING

There are three aspects to confident thinking that will help you be a master. The Three Ps of confident thinking are positive, process, and present.

Positive

Positive confident thinking means that you talk to yourself the same way you would talk to a teammate. A good player will try to keep their teammate in the BOX with words of encouragement. You would never say, "Dude you're killing us. You shouldn't be allowed to shoot anymore." Instead, you'd build him up. "Don't worry about it," you'd say. "You're good. You got this."

Talk to yourself the same way. I call this having a teammate mentality. Use the same positive, encouraging tone. Don't say, "I can't believe I missed that shot. I stink." Instead, remember it's just a minor setback and tell yourself, *I've got this. I'm good. Let's go.*

Anchor your thoughts to something undeniable and rooted in reality, such as your physical and technical gears. Tell yourself something like, *I've worked my butt off in practice this week. I've been nailing it. I've been a beast in the weight room. I've got this.* Your confidence builds because you know this to be true: you had a great week and worked hard.

Positive, confident thinking sidesteps any focus on the negative. Negative statements cause the brain to react with anxiety, while positive statements keep you more calm, self-assured, and focused. Say what you want instead of what you don't want. For example, instead of thinking *Don't strike out,* think *Swing at strikes,* or *Drive the ball.* The positive phrase is actionable and feels like it is more in your control.

Process

Process refers to how you think about and approach the controllable aspects of the game and what you must do to get the outcome you want.

You want to win, of course, but that result is largely out of your hands. Very few athletes, even the great ones, can direct final outcomes. There are too many uncontrollable variables that determine the final score. Focusing on winning can cause tension, and you want to avoid that. It is also a distraction because its focus is in the future.

Instead, concentrate on what you must do to win. Execute the game plan. Play with energy. Those are things you can control, and doing them will directly influence whether you win or lose. If you lose, you can find some consolation in knowing you did everything within your power to win. You controlled your controllables. You did your job. And that in itself is a victory.

Thinking about process keeps you anchored and directs your actions in a productive and determined way. Before shooting a free throw, former NBA star Adrian Dantley would stand at the line and say, "Over the front rim, back-spin, follow through." He was reminding himself of the process that would produce the outcome he needed—making the free throw. He was also keeping himself in the BOX. Dantley made 82 percent of his free throws over the course of his career and was inducted into the Basketball Hall of Fame in 2008. I'd say his thought process worked well.

CONTROL THE CONTROLLABLES: PROCESS AND OUTCOMES

A component of confident thinking is emphasizing process over outcome. You often cannot control the outcome, but you can control the process. If you emphasize process over outcome, you can still come away from a loss with the satisfaction that you did everything you could. The following are examples of processes athletes follow in order to achieve a particular outcome.

Process (what you do)	Outcome (what you want)
Shoot when open	Score
Attack the fastball	Get a hit
Execute game plan	Win
Box out aggressively	Get rebound
Follow my plan	Race well
Be disciplined	Avoid penalties
Move my feet	Play good defense
Play my game	Play well
Have fun	Have fun

Present

Confident athletes understand the value of staying in the present moment. They focus on what is happening right now and what they need to do to react to what is happening. Being present means you aren't thinking about anything except what is right in front of you. You aren't thinking about your last race, when a cramp slowed you down, and you aren't contemplating potential outcomes, such as finding yourself with too little gas for the final sprint.

Leaving the moment to worry about an uncertain future or to revisit an unpleasant past is what I call time traveling, and time traveling takes you to the Land of What-If. You become lost in thoughts like *What if I mess up?* or *What if we lose?* Or you might be time traveling backward and saying, "I played terribly in the last game," or "I remember when this team beat us last year." Time traveling causes anxiety because it shifts your focus to situations over which you had or have no control. You can't change what happened in the past, and what happens in the future is out of your control. So why think about those things?

On the other hand, staying in the present gives you a lot of control. When you're behind in the count 0–2, instead of worrying about striking out, concentrate on the upcoming pitch. Think *protect the plate* or *make contact*. Focusing on these *what nows* and not the *what-ifs* strips away the distractions and allows you to unleash your technical and physical attributes. The pitch is outside, so you let it go. That last pitch leaves the BOX and you turn your attention to the next pitch, ready to drive the ball if it's a strike.

CONFIDENT BEHAVIOR

While upbeat, purposeful, and present-moment thinking lead to confidence, certain behaviors—including pace, posture, actions, and overall demeanor—also play a role in keeping you in the BOX. For example, a golfer who hits a poor shot may walk more slowly to the next shot, her shoulders slumped and her fists clenched. Her brain notices the change in the golfer's posture, registers that there's a problem, and immediately starts analyzing why this is happening, bringing all kinds of what-ifs into the BOX.

However, if the golfer is aware of how her behavior and posture change after a bad shot, she's empowered to say, "Same approach. Same tempo. Go hit a great shot." When you know yourself, you play more deliberately, choose behaviors that boost your confidence, and stay inside the BOX.

Not every BOX looks the same. Each athlete's BOX varies based on their personality and a host of other factors. For example, LeBron James's BOX looks a lot different than Tim Duncan's. Both are great NBA players, but each had a strikingly different approach to the game. If Duncan tried to play like James, putting on a mean face, occupying more space on the court, or acting in an intimidating manner, he would not perform at his peak. In fact, it would be obvious to everyone in the arena that Tim Duncan, a quiet, stoic, and unflashy star, had exited the BOX. Similarly, LeBron's game would suffer if he tried to play a more reserved and controlled game like Duncan's.

The only one who knows what it feels like for you in the BOX is *you*. Think about the details of the best game you ever played. What was your warm-up like? Were you methodical and serious, or were you loose and relaxed, joking with your teammates? What did you do before the game? How did you get ready? What did you do to feel relaxed and confident during the game? Did you interact a lot with your teammates? How? When you were out of the game, what did you do from the sidelines to stay engaged in the action?

Try to completely paint the picture. As you do this, you develop your approach, or what you need to *do* to get into the BOX. You also develop ideas for how to react when you struggle and get knocked out of the BOX. If you are normally a happy kid on the court but find yourself down after a bad play, you know you've got to get back to the approach that you started with. Force a smile back on your face, and remind yourself that you play your best when you're having fun. Your confidence will catch up.

Once you know what works for you—including your energy level, style, and the activities that help you prepare for play—you can design an approach that works for you. The brain responds well to rituals and routines. When you come to a game with consistent thoughts and behaviors, the brain recognizes that it's time to get into the BOX and play.

DEVELOPING SELF-AWARENESS

Successful athletes reach a level of self-awareness that has three parts: an athletic identity, a job description, and a clear sense of approach.

You need to *know* who you are in order to *be* who you are. This is your athletic identity. When you're self-aware, you can emphasize your own strengths and not get distracted by the strengths of your opponents. It's neither necessary nor helpful to compare yourself to others, but it's vital that you know your own strengths and what your team needs from you. In other words, if your greatest skill is boxing out and grabbing rebounds, you don't drift out to the perimeter and start launching threes.

Your athletic identity helps you get a clear sense of your

job on the field or on the court. Determine the two or three things you must do for it to be a good game for you and your team. Tie your identity and your job together. For example, a player might say, "I'm a strong and physical player with excellent rebounding skills. My job is to play a physical game and be active on the boards at both ends of the court." In this way, your identity and your job are foremost in your mind when play begins.

After you define your identity and job, structure an approach that helps you stay in the BOX and get that job done. We can turn to Tim Duncan again for an example. Duncan's approach to professional basketball was to play with a practiced, deliberate style that relied on sound fundamentals and a dispassionate demeanor. He never played with freewheeling abandon the way many stars do, but that didn't seem to hold him back: he played nineteen seasons, all for the San Antonio Spurs, averaged nineteen points per game, and won five NBA championships.

Luke, the basketball player we talked about at the beginning of this chapter, also developed all of the elements of self-awareness—athletic identity, job description, and approach—as he sought to solve his performance issues. In time, his self-awareness helped him get back into the BOX and enjoy basketball again. Here's how.

Luke agreed his timidity and anxiety during games

stemmed from an undeveloped mental gear. He quickly saw that he needed to bulk up his mental approach so it was as fit and effective as his technical and physical abilities.

At first, he struggled to figure out his athletic identity. He was the only sophomore on the varsity team and wasn't sure how he fit in. However, in thinking about it and paying attention to what he brought to the team in practice, he realized that his team needed him to be not only athletic and energetic, but also multidimensional. He was not the team's best shooter, but he was a good shooter, and his team needed him to take the shot when he was open. He could also drive, defend, and pass. He could handle the ball. His team, he realized, needed him to do each of those things when the situation called for it. Over time, he was able to acknowledge everything he brought to the team, and as a result, he developed a powerful sense of his identity as a player. He was a versatile, multidimensional player.

Then Luke considered the question, "What's my job?" How could he help the team the most? He came to think of himself as a catalyst—a player who brought athletic energy to the court and made good things happen by stealing the ball, blocking shots, and filling the lane on fast breaks. He knew his teammates needed him at both ends of the court. They needed him to score if given the opportunity and they needed him to lock down the opponent's best player defensively. "I need to be out there and be a catalyst. I need to be athletic, get up and down the floor, make things happen," he told me. "When an opportunity to score arises, I need to take it."

Once Luke's job and identity were clear, he worked on defining his approach. He started by describing what it's like when he is playing great basketball. "I'll be flying around, having fun," he said. "You'll see me smiling, talking, and interacting with teammates. I'm diving for balls and not thinking very much."

As we were talking about this, he realized how much he'd been standing around, worrying about making a mistake. He also realized why his approach needed to be more freewheeling and energetic. That kind of play was natural for him and what his team needed.

Luke now understood his identity, his job, and how to approach the game. He was ready to go out there and be himself and do his job in his own way. That got him out of his head and allowed him to do what he knew he was capable of.

Luke also learned the value of changing his mindset. Where he had once spent a lot of time before games feeling anxious and worried about making mistakes, now he used his new self-awareness as an anchor. "I'm just going out there, being me, doing my job," he told himself, "and doing it my way." This new, positive focus was much better than his previous negative self-talk: "Don't screw up."

Luke also developed a pregame routine that prepared him to have a great game. He realized he needed to stay loose and not think too much about the game, so he focused on having fun and hanging with his teammates. When his coach said it was time to go to the locker room, Luke would put on his headphones and listen to a playlist he'd created. He directed his thinking to such positive affirmations as *I'm ready* and *I'm here for a reason* and *I'm gonna have a great game*. If he was feeling anxious, he would reframe his emotions and think of the anxiety as excitement instead of worry. He would use his breathing to settle himself down. When it was time to take the court, he would say to himself, "Be you, do your job, and do it your way." When warm-ups began, he made sure that his energy and tempo were both set to high.

Most importantly, Luke realized what it felt like when he was in the BOX. He said it is "a combination of excitement and calmness." He was relaxed because he was confident and excited because that's how he plays.

Luke improved his play as the season went on. By his

junior and senior years, he was clearly the emotional leader of his team, which won two championships. After high school, he went on to play basketball at a Division I program.

YOUR JOURNEY

Developing confidence and self-awareness does not happen overnight. It takes time to incorporate new thoughts, actions, and routines into your approach to competition. You're building a new habit of thinking. However, the more you work on building your confidence, developing your self-awareness, and putting both into your practices, games, and game preparation, the quicker they will take hold and the sooner you will see the results. At some point, you will cross that line and have a completely new mindset that works well for you.

CHAPTER 3

· · · · ·

MINDSET

The greatest efforts in sports come when the mind is as still as a glass lake.

—TIMOTHY GALLWEY

Make sure your worst enemy doesn't live between your own two ears.

—LAIRD HAMILTON

Mindset is the ability to control and direct your thoughts in a challenging moment. When you turn the ball over or make an error, you can either dwell on it with regret or anger and allow the event to distract you, or you can direct your thoughts in a way that maintains your confidence and allows you to focus on the next play. The *only* play that matters.

There are three facets to mindset:

1. Setting the mind
2. Settling the mind
3. Anchoring the mind

In this chapter, we take a closer look at each of these, beginning with the stories of three athletes.

TYLER: PRE-RACE ANXIETY

I met Tyler the summer before his senior year in high school. He was an outstanding swimmer on a team that was the reigning state champion. He had been swimming competitively since he was young, and his ability and work ethic had led to success at every level. For as long as he could remember, Tyler's goal was to swim in college, and several excellent programs were recruiting him.

Tyler's problem was not in the pool. He liked swim meets and being on the team, and he swam well once he hit the water. His problems arose before his races. As he waited for his heat to be called to the starting blocks, he was miserable. He knew he should be getting mentally prepared for his race, but instead he was filled with anxiety and dread. His thoughts sped up and would bounce around his head like the steel ball in a pinball machine. He imagined all kinds of unlikely scenarios, such as being unable to finish the race or missing a turn. He frequently felt physically sick before a race. It had gotten so bad that he was thinking of giving up college opportunities because he felt that four more years of feeling this way would make him miserable.

Tyler desperately needed tools to settle into the BOX before he competed.

MACKENZIE: LOSING FOCUS IN GAMES

Mackenzie was a high school freshman volleyball player who was moved up to varsity to be groomed as the team's *libero*—the defensive specialist who wears a different color jersey than the rest of the team and doesn't serve or rotate to the front line.

Mackenzie was a quick, coordinated player who understood the game and the role her coach wanted her to play. But her coach said she often "got lost" during matches and seemed to remain distracted after mistakes. Mackenzie agreed. She said she often played tentatively during a match because she worried about "messing up" and either disappointing her teammates or causing her team to lose. This was *not* how a libero should play.

Mackenzie needed tools to set her thoughts and help her get into the BOX. She needed to control her reactions in games and narrow her thinking so she could do her job.

JAMES: LOSING HIS LOVE OF THE GAME

James was a golfer. He loved the sport and had been playing since he was ten years old. He was one of the better players on his high school team, often posting scores that contributed to team victories and occasionally winning "medalist" honors for the lowest score.

However, during his junior year, James started falling apart in tournaments and matches. If he hit a bad shot, he would berate himself and undermine his confidence and focus by muttering things like, "It's not that hard, stupid. Just hit the shot." James was a gas-on athlete; a mistake would make him feel an urgency to make up for past shots, and this only led to more errors. He'd rush putts and would swing for every green instead of laying up and playing for the par.

By the time I met James, he seemed to have lost his love of the sport. He was embarrassed and frustrated. He was on the verge of quitting golf.

"The worst part of all this," James said, "is that I really do love golf. I've played it since I was a kid. I've always loved it. I thought it was something I would play for the rest of my life, but now it's making me crazy."

James needed to remember why he loved golf and get back to playing the game rather than fighting it. He needed to anchor himself to a personal sports philosophy that was realistic, respected the game, and freed him to get back to having fun (and playing well).

THE THREE FACETS OF MINDSET

Tyler, Mackenzie, and James all had issues with their mindset—or how their thinking affected their play. They needed to understand how their thoughts changed their game, so they could learn to control and direct their thinking in a way that optimized their performance rather than compromising it. They needed to understand and work on mastering the three facets of mindset: setting, settling, and anchoring.

SETTING THE MIND

Setting the mind refers to how you use your thinking to put yourself into the BOX before competing. Think of it as a mental warm-up.

Athletes don't just show up at game time or race time and say, "Let's do this." They want to perform well, so they make sure they're warmed up and ready. However, these warm-ups typically ignore the mental gear and focus on getting the body loose and the skills sharp. Baseball and softball players, for example, often start their warm-ups by stretching and doing some running in the outfield.

They do some long tosses to loosen their throwing arms. Then they move into skill-specific warm-ups like hitting in the cage and taking ground balls.

Similarly, tennis players begin by stretching and running to warm up their muscles. Then they take to the court to make sure their serving, groundstrokes, and volleying skills are ready. These kinds of warm-ups are designed to lubricate your physical and technical gears.

You must also warm up your mental gear. You don't want to start out "flat" or "freaked." You want to be in the BOX when it's time to compete.

An excellent mental routine works in concert with the rest of your warm-up. Your mental warm-up is designed to narrow your thoughts and foster your confidence. It prepares you to step into the BOX when the whistle blows.

Resetting works the same way. There may be times during a game when one of the "dis-es" gets you and you find yourself out of the BOX. It happens to every athlete. When it does, you can use a timeout, or the time between the first and second halves of a game to redirect your thoughts to your pregame routine and the thinking that works for you. When play resumes, you are back in the BOX and ready to have an outstanding second half.

SETTLING THE MIND

Settling is regaining access to your thoughts. This is particularly important during big games and dramatic moments within any game. If something goes wrong and you become distracted or discouraged, you need tools—such as a deep breath or two—to prevent anxiety and panicky feelings from taking over. You suspend your thinking until you settle down, regain access to your thoughts, and can rationally direct your mind again.

Imagine you are playing in a championship basketball game. The game is tied late in the fourth quarter, and you're fouled at the defensive end. The other team is in a penalty situation, which means you will be shooting foul shots. The crowd explodes, half of them pleading with you to hit both free throws, and the rest of the crowd booing the foul call and hoping you'll miss. You are swept away by the crowd noise and the intensity of the moment.

During the walk to the other end of the court, you must settle yourself. You must deflect all thoughts from the BOX that are clamoring to get in—*What if I miss these shots? I can't let my teammates down!*—so you can focus on your process. Settling your mind is like finding the eye of the hurricane. You quiet your thoughts and calm your emotions. You relax your muscles. By slowing down and taking a breath to calm your mind, you also settle your body. You feel your shoulders loosen so you can execute your technical skills with grace and fluidity. By the time you settle in at the foul line, you can think about the free throw in the same way you think of every free throw.

You smoothly execute your shot like you have hundreds of times before. Swish. Swish. Win!

ANCHORING THE MIND

Anchoring is about connecting yourself to a realistic and positive philosophy with respect to your sport and yourself as a competitive athlete. This is your *sports credo*. Anchoring helps athletes avoid slipping into the unrealistic expectations and harsh judgments that hinder performance and steal joy from the game.

Developing your anchor requires some self-reflection. Ask yourself why you play the sport. Why do you love the sport? How do you play when you're at your best? What aspects of your sport frustrate you, and how do you want to handle those? What would you like to be able to say to yourself after every game? A personal philosophy can help you with the demands of being a competitive athlete and guide you through the ups and downs of playing at a high level.

Your personal philosophy should be based on realistic expectations. For instance, it's not realistic to think you will never lose, yet some athletes continue to react like the world is coming to an end after a loss. An anchoring philosophy for these athletes might be this: *I play to win but accept that it won't always happen. And when it doesn't, I use the loss to get better.* Their philosophy might also acknowledge that there will be times for every athlete when they won't play as well as they want to or are outplayed by an opponent. Being realistic about this keeps them from becoming overly discouraged and losing confidence.

Another aspect of your personal philosophy is understanding how you show respect for the sport, for yourself, and for your opponents. This acknowledges that mastering a sport is difficult. Elite golfers spend years practicing with the goal of shooting par or subpar rounds. Despite this commitment, even professionals make bogey or double bogey regularly. When you react negatively to a bad shot or to posting a big number on a hole—whether in action or word—you are not showing respect for your sport. You are undermining your confidence and inviting emotion into the BOX. Making a twelve-foot putt is challenging, and overreacting when you miss one suggests it's easy. It isn't.

Reacting with anger also pushes you out of the BOX and makes it more likely you will continue to grind your way around the golf course. It's natural to be upset after hitting a bad shot, but you have to accept that this is part of the game and clear the BOX for the next shot.

It's also vital that you respect your opponent when you lose. You may be disappointed in your performance, but it's important to acknowledge the accomplishment of those who beat you. They love the sport like you do, they practice hard like you do, and sometimes they will beat you. Will you act out or will you shake their hand? Staying aware of your philosophy—your anchor—will temper your reaction and help you respond in a way that respects the game and your opponent. It also helps you to grow as an athlete and enjoy your sport more.

PUTTING IT ALL TOGETHER

All facets of mindset are intimately tied to getting into the BOX, staying in the BOX, and returning to the BOX when you get knocked out by emotions or pulled out by a distraction.

Setting the mind with a mental precompetition routine is how you access the BOX from the start. When you think the right thoughts and do the right things to be mentally prepared, your mental gear is as warmed up as your physical and technical gears.

Settling the mind keeps you in the BOX or lets you back

in during moments of high pressure and intensity. When you regulate and control your emotions, you can manage your nerves and regain focus in a way that increases your energy and gets you back to optimal play.

Anchoring yourself in a personal philosophy can help keep you from getting knocked out of the BOX when adverse events occur. You are more likely to stay in the BOX and enjoy competing if you avoid criticizing or judging yourself and learn to handle the inevitable challenges and setbacks that come from being a competitive athlete at a high level.

CREATING EFFECTIVE PREGAME ROUTINES

The brain loves routines. Routines calm and focus the mind and send a clear signal that it's time to get ready. And routines can be designed to have a specific outcome at a specified time. A warm-up routine, for example, can tell your brain to get ready for competition.

Michael Phelps is known for doing the same things 120 minutes before his race, 90 minutes before his race, 45 minutes before his race, and 25 minutes before his race. He approaches every race in the same way. Teams also often have routines or rituals that send a clear mental signal that it's time to play, like praying in the locker room, or tapping the "Play Like a Champion Today" sign, or circling around an inspirational leader for a pregame motivational speech.

> ## CREATING YOUR PREGAME ROUTINE
>
> Athletes should develop and commit to a pregame routine that starts the day of the competition.
>
> - Begin with positive thinking that creates excitement and anticipation—*It's gonna be a great day. I can't wait to play!*
>
> - Develop a routine for the time before you leave for your game, like eating the same snack and doing the same thing to relax.
>
> - Create a routine that works best for you for when you arrive for your game. Do you enjoy relaxing with teammates, or would you rather be alone listening to a pregame playlist?
>
> - What kind of thoughts might contribute to your mental warm-up? Focus on your job, identity, and approach. Narrow your thinking to what you need to do during the competition and how you will do it. Consider using some mental imagery to "see" yourself playing great.
>
> When you direct and focus your thinking in this way, you create your perfect mindset. By game time you are ready to step into the BOX, play to your strengths, and do what you need to do.

TOOLS TO LEVERAGE

Connecting your mindset to tools that regulate your emotions is essential. Breathing is one of the easiest and best tools. Taking a few deep breaths before stepping to the plate, getting into the blocks, or taking a penalty kick allows your mind to settle and helps your muscles relax so they can work in unison and deliver optimal performance.

There is a lot of downtime for athletes—before games, between games, traveling to games. There are times when the pressure and grind of competing at a high level create physical and emotional stress, which can lead to anxious thoughts. Every competitive athlete needs tools for these times. Some read, listen to music, play video games, or stream movies. Sometimes the stress can build and become uncomfortable for athletes (or anyone). For these times, I recommend they practice mindfulness or meditation. Both are excellent ways to relax and keep the pressures from building up.

Mindfulness is merely being fully present in the moment and directing your awareness to a single focal point while blocking out everything else. It can be as simple as focusing on your breath, your body, or a single object. There are some excellent mindfulness apps for smartphones, and I encourage every athlete I work with, especially athletes with significant travel, to find one that works well for them.

MINDFUL OBSERVATION

This is a simple mindfulness exercise that can be done wherever you are to slow yourself down and get reconnected to the present moment. Five minutes is all the time you'll need (a timer can be helpful).

1. Choose a single object from wherever you are—something in the room you're in or on the other side of a window. Focus your attention on the object and merely observe it.

2. As you look at the object, allow yourself to relax. If other thoughts enter your mind, just let them pass and redirect yourself to the object.

3. Look at this object like it's the first time you've ever seen it. Notice details that might escape the attention of someone looking at it casually.

4. When the time is up, notice how calm you feel. Become aware of the pace of your breathing and how relaxed your muscles are. Now you're ready for whatever comes next.

TYLER, MACKENZIE, AND JAMES

All three of the athletes from the beginning of the chapter had problems with their mindset, and each developed a different approach to solving their problem.

To control his performance anxiety, Tyler developed tools to settle his mind. He learned to slow down his thinking and reduce his anxiety with breathing techniques. He also practiced mindfulness meditation, picking out an object or a scene and focusing on it to the exclusion of everything else.

Tyler designed a routine that started thirty minutes before his race. He found a quiet place—by the diving pool or somewhere else away from the main competition pool—and spent ten minutes gazing at the water while listening to a relaxing playlist. This kept him calm and relaxed as he got closer to race time. After ten minutes of meditative calm, Tyler started a dynamic warm-up and switched to a playlist consisting of more upbeat, motivational music. He wouldn't let his thoughts stray to the what-ifs (*What if I'm slow off the blocks?*) or the things outside his control (*Why did they put me in lane eight? I hate swimming in an outside lane*). Instead, Tyler concentrated on his process—start strong, maintain your pace, empty the tank on the last fifty. He stayed grounded in this way for another fifteen minutes.

For the last five minutes, Tyler changed the music to his favorite motivational song and repeated a mantra that he developed for himself: "Get wet, swim fast, enjoy the ride." He allowed nothing into his mind but positive thoughts and powerful images of himself slicing through the water. When the song ended, he walked to the blocks.

Tyler is currently swimming in college and having fun doing it.

Mackenzie learned that she couldn't start thinking about a match too early. Contemplating an upcoming match made her anxious, so she pushed thoughts of competition out of her head. Instead, she hung out with friends until the coach said it was time to get ready to play.

Her pregame routine kicked in immediately before the match. It started with positive self-talk, like "I'm ready. I've had a great week of practice. I've worked really hard." She thought of the match as a reward, and this allowed her to just go out and have fun. She intentionally thought about how she should play and what her goals were. (*Okay, what have we been working on? What's the game plan? What do we need to execute?*) She thought about what the coach said she should focus on during the match.

Right before the match, she transitioned her thoughts again and reminded herself to go out and do her job: dig and pass. She kept her thoughts contained and narrowly focused on her role. On the court, she visualized a square in front of her. Before every ball was put in play, she would step forward into the square. "Stepping into the BOX," as she would put it, was her behavioral cue that connected with the thought *Right here, right now.* Mackenzie no longer struggled with overthinking or getting "lost" during games.

As a junior, Mackenzie was the starting libero on her volleyball team.

James rekindled his love of golf by writing out his personal philosophy as an anchor. He contemplated questions such as: *Why do I love golf? How do I play my best? What's my goal for a round of golf that's not an outcome like winning or scoring? What are the difficult and challenging aspects of golf? How do I want to handle setbacks and disappointments on the course? How do I show respect for myself and the game? When I finish a round, what do I want to be able to say to myself?*

He wrote out his sports credo and kept it folded up in his golf bag so he would see it during play. It served as a reminder. This is what he wrote:

> "I love golf because it's fun, challenging, and you get to play on beautiful courses with your friends. My goal is to play well, not perfectly. I know that I will play my best when I have fun, trust my game, and commit myself to play one shot at a time. I believe that I can hit a great shot every time I stand over the ball, but I also accept the fact that I won't hit a great shot every time. I know that getting angry with myself after a poor shot never helps and takes away the fun. When I finish a round, I want to be able to say I gave it my best, competed on every hole, and had fun."

This credo helped James remain grounded when he played. It reestablished a perspective that made golf fun again and helped him manage both his expectations and his reactions to bad shots or holes. He stopped fighting the game and got back to just playing it. And, not surprisingly, he got back to playing it well.

For help in developing your own sports credo, turn to Worksheet #15 ("Play Grounded") in Chapter 7. You'll find another example of a sports credo as well as an outline that will help you write your own.

DESIGN YOUR OWN PROCESS

Each of these athletes found a different challenge related to mindset. One had trouble setting her mind during games, another needed to settle his mind before races, and the third needed an anchor to remind him why he loved his sport.

If you have trouble controlling and directing your thoughts in difficult moments, you may need help in one or more of these areas. The key to mastering mindset is to focus on your process and the things that you can control, develop useful routines, and practice the art of keeping distracting or discouraging thoughts out of the BOX by controlling your breathing and using mindfulness techniques. It helps, too, to have thought through and composed your own convictions about your sport, what draws you to it, and how you want to play it.

Mindset, like confidence, resilience, and emotions, helps you get into the BOX and stay there, or get back in when negative or distracting thoughts throw you out. Another key to that process is learning how to control your emotions, so let's move on to the next chapter and talk about how to handle that challenge.

CHAPTER 4

· · · · ·

EMOTIONS

A ballplayer who loses his head and can't keep his cool is worse than no player at all.

—LOU GEHRIG

Learn to control your emotions or they will control you.

—EDGAR MARTINEZ

Emotions run high in athletics. The anticipation, tension, and struggle can elicit great joy or deep sadness. If you play sports, you've probably felt a variety of emotions across this spectrum. You're at the foul line with the score tied and just a few seconds left. *Tension.* You're at the plate and the count is 3–2 in the bottom of the ninth with the score tied. *Excitement.* You're closing in on the frontrunner with only a hundred yards left in the race. *Determination.*

Emotion is why we love sports. But it's also the primary reason athletes get knocked out of the BOX.

Athletes who don't learn how to control their emotions have a hard time staying focused. Some athletes feel too much, which makes them move too fast or go too hard, and some athletes have the opposite response, and their performance becomes too slow and tentative. Erin and Michael are examples of how these different types of reactions can both disrupt an athlete's performance.

GAS ON

Erin was a fourteen-year-old tennis player. Her goal was to earn a Division I tennis scholarship and go on to play professionally. She knew what she wanted and worked hard to get it. She worked out with a personal trainer, took private lessons from a professional, and played on a club team that practiced five days a week. She played a lot of high-level tournaments against other talented players.

Erin was fast and strong, had plenty of endurance, and was highly skilled; she had a wicked serve and graceful groundstrokes. She was like an octopus with eight arms at the net, getting her racket on every shot that came her way.

Her only flaw was her temper. If she missed an easy shot

or a lob drifted out of bounds, her anger would rise up and take over. She understood the importance of consistency in tennis, but when she missed shots she should have made, she sometimes became unhinged. She was like an artist who had carefully carved a beautiful sculpture and then accidentally knocked it over with one awkward gesture, shattering the work into a thousand pieces. "Sometimes I'd be playing great, and then I'd just lose it," she told me. "I don't know what happens, but it's not pretty."

Erin's mom believed that her competitiveness was a double-edged sword. Erin played with a fierce intensity, which helped her win, but that intensity could also be strong enough to knock her out of the BOX. According to her mom, the "wheels would come off."

Erin's game would change dramatically after a mistake. She would go from her usual game of hitting beautifully varied shots to pounding every ball over the net as hard as she could. One error would be compounded by the next, and all the while, her anger would grow inside her. Occasionally, she'd throw her racket in rage. "When it gets to that point," she told me, "I'm just kind of waiting to get the match over with."

Erin's problem wasn't consistency; she didn't make more mistakes than most other good tennis players. She just let those mistakes bother her more. She let her emotion shove her out of the BOX. Erin's anger and intense emotions—and her inability to deal with them—made it difficult for her to access her highly developed technical and physical gears.

Erin's emotional response to disruptive events was a *gas-on* response. When she got knocked out of the BOX, she hit the accelerator and sped up, always chasing the mistake to fix it or get even.

GAS OFF

Michael was a three-sport athlete, playing soccer in the fall, basketball in the winter, and baseball in the spring and summer.

Although he was a talented and well-rounded baseball player—he could pitch as well as play many other positions in the field—his parents thought Michael was often too hard on himself. When he didn't play well or made a mistake on the field, he became gloomy and withdrawn.

During one game, for example, Michael played very well for several innings, collecting a few hits and making some outstanding plays in the field. His team was ahead, thanks in part to Michael's excellent play. In the last inning, with his team ahead by three runs, his coach brought Michael in to pitch. Michael had closed out a lot of games in this way.

Michael struck out the first batter and got the second hitter to ground out weakly to short. Two outs. Last inning. Three-run lead. One of the team's best pitchers on the mound. Piece of cake, right?

Unfortunately, Michael's next pitch sailed inside and hit the batter.

Michael's mom, sitting in the bleachers, could see an immediate change in her son. As Michael watched the batter trot down to first base, tears seemed to well up in his eyes.

The coach went to the mound to help his pitcher settle down, but Michael asked to be taken out of the game. The coach reminded Michael that they had a good lead. Michael just needed to relax and pitch his game. The coach left Michael in.

Michael's next several pitches were significantly slower and way out of the strike zone. He walked the next three batters before the coach finally pulled him before he could walk in another run.

After leaving the game, Michael went to the end of the

dugout bench, pulled his hat down low over his eyes, and completely disconnected from his teammates, not speaking or acknowledging anyone. A reliever came in and got the last out, but even as his teammates celebrated the victory, there was no joy in the win for Michael. He felt he'd let his teammates down and embarrassed himself.

Like Erin, Michael's emotions had jammed up his other gears. His muscle memory, developed by countless hours of practice and training, hadn't disappeared, but it was compromised. Compromised by his emotion. Michael's reaction to an adverse event (hitting a batter) impaired his competitive thinking. He began worrying about what his teammates were thinking and whether his poor pitching might cause his team to lose. These thoughts created pressure. He responded to this pressure by slowing down and becoming tentative. Instead of concentrating on the only thing he could control—the next pitch—he worried about what-ifs and "blowing it."

Michael's response was typical of a *gas-off* reaction. He was overthinking the errant pitch. While Erin's reaction had been to speed up and commit more mistakes, Michael's mental gear began to turn more slowly, disrupting and stalling his physical and technical gears.

Regardless of which end of the spectrum you fall on— whether you're a *gas-on* or a *gas-off* type—an overly emotional response to a disruptive event will affect your performance. Psychologists describe this as a "flight or fight" response because primitive people, when faced with something emotionally or physically frightening, like doing battle with a saber-toothed tiger, had a choice to either stand and fight or to flee. Either way, the body releases hormones that prepare you to do one or the other.

Although we are no longer primitive people, we all experience the flight or fight symptoms when confronted by a big, growling dog or when we're called on to give an oral presentation at school or work. Our heartbeat speeds up, our breathing becomes shallower, and our muscles tense up. This might be helpful for survival, but it is not good for performance.

Gas on is like the "fight" response—you chase the mistake and strain to overcome it. Gas off is more like the "flight" response—you try to escape the issue by overthinking the situation and exercising extreme caution. Either way, the secret is to recognize that what is happening to you is not going to help your present situation at all. In fact, you're not running from or preparing to do battle with a saber-toothed tiger at all; you're just playing sports. There is no need to overreact. The better you are at quickly realizing this, the faster you can get back into the BOX, return to the level of play you're capable of, and start having fun again.

MANAGING EMOTIONS

Emotions are unavoidable. They are a part of the human condition and a natural byproduct of being an athlete. Nothing's better than the thrill of victory, and nothing can feel worse than the agony of defeat.

The energy generated by emotion can either enhance performance or get in the way of it. The key is to direct that emotional energy appropriately. Once you understand how emotions affect performance, you can manage them to produce a positive outcome. You can use emotion to sharpen your focus and increase the intensity of your game. A channeled emotional response can give you extra energy when your tank is empty.

The story of the US hockey team's gold medal in the 1980 Winter Olympics at Lake Placid, called the "Miracle on Ice," is an excellent example of how emotions had a positive impact and elevated a team's play. The Soviet Union's hockey team had won the last four Olympic gold medals (and five of the last six) and were the overwhelming favorites to win again in Lake Placid. The Soviets were primarily professional players who had extensive experience playing together internationally. The Americans, on the other hand, were the youngest team in the tournament, and none of the players were professionals. They also didn't have much experience playing together.

However, the US team was playing on its home ice, and the emotion and patriotism swept them along to an unexpected victory. They beat the Soviets in the first game of the medal round, coming from behind to win 4–3 in one of the greatest upsets in sports history. Then they went on to defeat Finland to win the gold medal. If you saw the game or even the movie about the game, there's no doubt that the high emotional pitch felt by the players in that Olympics helped the US athletes perform at a higher level than anyone had expected them to.

Not all athletes are good at managing the emotions inherent in competitive play, however. A gas-on response like Erin's may cause emotions to *push* you out of the BOX if anger or frustration tricks you into playing too aggressively as you scramble to make up for your mistake. You are distracted by fear and anger. Alternatively, a gas-off response like Michael's may let anxiety *pull* you out of the BOX.

To determine if emotions are knocking you out of the BOX, think about how your performance is affected by disruptive events. For example, say you are playing tennis and your opponent is cheating by calling your baseline shots out, even though you can see they are in. How do you react? Do you start drilling every shot back across the net with hostile force, or do you calmly begin mixing in some drop shots and lobs? If you're doing the latter, you are processing your anger efficiently and converting it into energy and focus. It's safe to say you productively managed your emotion and stayed in the BOX.

Managing emotions is essential any time your performance slips due to a disruptive event—the *dis*traction of a cheating opponent, the *dis*appointment of missing a penalty kick, or the *dis*couragement of not playing much in the first half. Being overly critical or thinking about the event negatively leads to distorted emotions and the gas-on or gas-off response.

Some athletes can harness their emotions in ways that don't have a dramatic effect on how they play, but their feelings still steal their enjoyment of the sport. For example, you may win an eight-hundred-meter race but still feel disappointed because you didn't run your best time. Your performance is outstanding, and the result is outstanding, but your emotions spoil your experience. This is an excellent time to remind yourself that it's supposed to be fun and you don't always run a personal best. Enjoy your victory! This can work the other way, too. Some athletes can run or swim personal-best times but focus on the fact that they didn't win, creating a negative emotion that tarnishes a significant accomplishment. When you perform well, you should feel proud, regardless of the outcome.

If your emotions prevent you from having fun playing the

game you love, or if your feelings hurt your performance, you need to work on your mental gear.

FINDING THE EYE OF THE HURRICANE

When tension builds—the crowd is going crazy, you've made an error, or you're going into overtime—follow these steps to quickly calm yourself so you can focus on what you need to do.

1. Close your eyes and take a deep breath.

2. Exhale slowly through your lips. As you exhale, use positive self-talk, like "You're good" or "You've got this," to establish a positive mindset. Take a second breath if necessary.

3. Open your eyes and reconnect to the moment. It may still be crazy, but you're calm. Step back into the BOX and do what you need to do.

EMOTIONAL CRUISE CONTROL

There are three reactions to disruptive events. We've discussed how the first two, gas on and gas off, are problematic. The third option is to use your emotional cruise control to regulate extreme reactions and prevent them from undermining your performance.

You can train yourself to be aware of your unique emotional set point, or how you *feel* when you're in the BOX. This self-awareness will help you quickly realize when an emotion has taken you out of the BOX, so you can take immediate action to get back in. You can't prevent disruptive events from occurring, but you can learn to maintain or restore your emotional equilibrium when they do.

When you are aware of your ideal emotional speed, you know where to set your emotional cruise control. Just as a driver may purposefully override the cruise control to pass another vehicle, an athlete may allow emotion to accelerate their play or fuel a competitive burst. For example, a football player may respond to being beaten by a wide receiver by making a great hustle play that saves a touchdown. However, in these situations, athletes need to use their awareness and tools to return to their emotional set point so they don't continue to play with heightened emotion that can become detrimental to their performance. If the football player continued to play angry, for example, he would be susceptible to mental mistakes.

It takes time and practice to train your responses when emotions are triggered. I would never tell an athlete, "Don't let it upset you." Athletes are human. They're also competitive. So instead, I would say, "Let's work on what you do when you get upset."

There's nothing terrible about emotion unless it's getting in your way. Athletes must learn to recognize when their feelings have pushed them from the BOX and know how to find their set point so they can quickly return to it. If your performance or experience is affected negatively, view it as an indicator that you need to work on the emotional mechanics.

OVERCOMING EMOTION

Emotions are not a character flaw. They are merely a part of your life and a part of the game. Just because you overreact or get embarrassed on the court doesn't mean you're mentally weak. It just says you have to work on your mental game in the same way you practice your shooting, blocking, or passing.

For example, when Michael hit a batter with a pitch and asked to be taken out of the game, he gave in to negative thinking. He thought his actions were unforgivable and that his teammates would hate him because they were bound to lose the game. The event led to negative emotions, which led to poor performance.

However, what if Michael had been able to rewrite the script in his head? What if he felt his teammates supported him despite his mistake? If Michael believed that his teammates still had faith in him because he had come through many times before, then he might have quickly returned to the BOX. His confidence in his physical and technical skills would have remained intact, and he would have resumed pitching without a trace of hesitation or tentativeness.

Developing this mental mechanic starts with self-awareness about the impact of your emotions on your game. Are you a gas-on or gas-off kind of player? How do you know when you're out of the BOX? When you understand the emotional responses that get you into trouble and the situations that trigger them, you can script new reactions that, with practice, will eventually become automatic, even in difficult conditions.

A technique to employ when your emotions spike and pop you out of the BOX is breathing. When you are anxious or upset, your breath becomes shallow and forced and signals to your brain that it's time for fight-or-flight behavior. Slow, deep breaths (abdominal breathing) that fill your lungs mimic the way we breathe when asleep and send a signal to the brain that it's all good, there's no crisis, carry on.

The next time you're scared or anxious, try using your breath to calm down. Take a big, controlled breath in, filling your lungs. Hold it until you feel a comfortable tension. Then breathe out through your mouth. Practice this technique every night, and you'll train your body how to relax immediately. The process will become so familiar that when you double fault or miss a wide open shot, you can literally use your breath to turn on the emotional cruise control. The breath is the perfect tool because it's always available.

Deep breath.

Slow down. ("You're good.")

Back in the BOX.

Next play.

ERIN'S SOLUTION

Erin knew her anger was unsportsmanlike, but she had not connected it to poor performance. With some reflection, she identified herself as a gas-on responder and even said, "The person who beats me the most is 'angry Erin,' so I need to work on that."

Erin's self-awareness was a significant first step because she made it a part of her prematch process. She had a mantra: "Don't let angry Erin beat you."

She also used breathing techniques. We developed a two-step breath exercise in which she would take a big inhalation followed by an exaggerated exhalation that let her visualize blowing out her anger. Then she'd take a second breath with a more relaxed exhalation to settle herself. She connected the second exhalation to a refocusing command: "next point." The idea is that the last point is history, the anger is history, and now it's time to get back into the BOX and play *this* point.

The breathing process helped Erin stop thinking about the past (the mistake that had angered her) or the future (how she was going to drill her next shot to make up for the mistake). Instead, the breathing and refocusing command helped her stay present and remain in the moment. All she thought about was the next point and what she needed to do to win it.

Erin also developed a process to remind her that the only shot that mattered was the present shot. After every point, she would bounce the ball three times before serving, then take a breath and move into the mechanics of serving the ball. If she was receiving the ball, she would tap her strings three times, take the same breath, and then set her feet to return the serve.

Committing to this process before every point made it difficult if not impossible for negative thoughts to interfere with Erin's performance. When a point was over, she merely repeated the routine, and the new point would begin.

MICHAEL'S SOLUTION

Michael also made the connection between poor performance and his emotional reactions. He had to get over his embarrassment and accept that this wasn't a personal weakness, just a game issue that he had to work on.

Like Erin, he started with breathing techniques. When something happened, he immediately instructed himself to take a deep breath and "slow down."

With my assistance, Michael "scouted" himself to become more aware of his triggers and vulnerabilities. With that knowledge, he was able to develop a personal game plan consisting of strategic responses designed to get better results. For example, if he hit someone with a pitch or any other disruptive event happened, he'd call timeout. He would then take a breath and bend down to retie his shoe. While tying his shoe, he would recite an affirmation to himself: "Trust, hard, fun," which was mental shorthand for "trust yourself, throw hard, have fun." When he finished, he took one more breath to settle himself. As he stepped on the mound, he imagined himself stepping back into the BOX, where there was only one pitch to think about—this pitch.

Erin and Michael both created a plan involving specific, concrete processes to keep them from overreacting to whatever just happened. They both reevaluated how they viewed being an athlete and how they thought about their respective sports. Once they accepted that a double fault or a bad pitch was simply an event that happened to every athlete, they were less prone to react emotionally and negatively when those things occurred. They realized that mistakes need not be thought of as horrible or unforgivable. Mistakes happen. You can't always control them, but you can control how you react to them.

Keep in mind that it takes time for any new process to become the equivalent of muscle memory. You may slip back into old patterns. However, if you can stay on the lookout for these patterns and catch yourself, you can redirect your thinking. Every time you recognize that you are out of the BOX and use tools to get back in, you are one step closer to creating a mental game as strong as the rest of your game. And one step closer to mastering the mental mechanic discussed in the next chapter—resilience.

CHAPTER 5

· · · · ·

RESILIENCE

No one plays this or any game perfectly. It's the guy who recovers from his mistakes who wins.

—PHIL JACKSON

Inside the ring or out, ain't nothing wrong with going down. It's staying down that's wrong.

—MUHAMMAD ALI

Even great athletes make mistakes. There's no free pass from bad breaks and adversity. Great athletes become great because they've learned to move quickly past their mistakes. They are resilient. They have astonishing physical and technical skills, but they also have the mental ability to continue to perform well in the face of disruptive events.

Stacey came to me after her freshman year of college

playing Division I golf. She was disappointed in her season and had decided to spend the summer developing her mental game.

Golf gives players a lot of time to think. Stacey realized this might be an issue for her.

Stacey experienced what she described as "mental lapses" during play. If she had a bad break, like hitting a tree branch or making a poor shot, she would struggle to get back on track for the next few holes. She was confident in her ability to make shots, but she had a tendency to exaggerate the importance of mishaps. She would overanalyze her play and ruminate about what had happened. Typical thoughts were *I knew I should have laid up,* or *I can't believe I hit that shot in the water.* She let her past mistakes linger in her mind, thinking, *That could end up costing me the match! Why did I do that? I have to make up for that.*

As Stacey played, she kept all of her thoughts about poor shots and bad breaks in the BOX with her, and each bad shot compromised the next. It became clear that the mental lapses she experienced when she played were due to her inability to bounce back from a setback.

She lacked resilience.

BOUNCING BACK

Resilience is the ability to empty the BOX so that the only play you think about is the one unfolding in the present. Resilient athletes make sure disruptive events don't impact what follows.

You can think of resilience on a micro level or a macro level. The micro level is shot to shot or play by play; an athlete shrugs off a lousy shot and empties the BOX before the next shot. The macro level refers to the ability to move on from a bad inning or a bad period or a bad game. An athlete has to be able to put a rough first half away and come out strong for the second half. A team has to get past the disappointment of a loss so they can focus on preparing for the next game. Slumps, both individual and team, often are the result of dragging the weight of poor performances forward.

Resilience is key to performance at the individual and the team level. Every team and every athlete is going to make mistakes and suffer disappointments, but the way they handle the missteps is what makes the difference. If you can move to the next play or the next game, you protect and maintain your confidence and focus, which is crucial to good performance.

A perfect example of resilience in action was the Chicago Cubs of 2016. It had been 108 years since the Cubs had won a World Series, but all season long they had dominated Major League Baseball on their way to a 103-win regular season. They marched through the playoffs before facing off against the Cleveland Indians in the World Series. Cubs fans were optimistic the team would go all the way, but even many diehard fans worried that the Cubs' history of failure would rise up and dash their hopes of a world championship.

The series against the Indians went to a seventh and decisive game, but the Cubs seemed to be in control, leading 5–1 and then 6–3. Then, in the bottom of the eighth inning, Cleveland's Rajai Davis hit a game-tying homer against Cubs closer Aroldis Chapman. The Chicago players and fans were stunned, with looks that seemed to say, "Is this really happening?" The game went into extra innings, but not before the game was delayed by a sudden downpour.

During the seventeen-minute delay, Cubs outfielder Jason Heyward called a team meeting and gave his teammates an impassioned speech about resilience.

"I know some things may have happened tonight you don't like," Heyward said, "but we're the best team in baseball, and we're the best team in baseball for a reason. Now we're going to show it. We play like the score is nothing-nothing. We've got to stay positive and fight for your brothers. Stick together, and we're going to win this game."

When the game resumed, the Cubs scored two runs in the top of the tenth and held on to win 8–7.

Heyward's clubhouse speech helped his team get back into the BOX. The Cubs and the Indians were both in a pressure cooker, but the Cubs' long history of futility surely brought additional anxiety to the Chicago dugout. Heyward reined that emotion in and ushered his team back to where they needed to be: focused on the present with confidence and purpose.

If you're hanging on to mistakes, the BOX becomes cluttered, and your thinking begins to time travel. This compromises your concentration and opens the door to negative emotion. You start to feel frustrated and discouraged, and your confidence wanes. For example, a struggling athlete may feel lost and overwhelmed by all of the plays accumulating and replaying in her head. She might be teeing off on number eight and still have the emotional echo of the three-putt on number seven in her head. She isn't focused on her shot, which is the only shot she has any control over. When certain plays "stick" in the BOX this way, they cause other gears to get jammed.

Good plays can get stuck as well. If you are still celebrating a great block or kill shot you just made, you're distracted from the current play, which needs all of your focus. It's also easy to get stuck thinking about the next play, as in *If I don't strike this guy out, I've got to face the cleanup batter.* You're bringing plays into the BOX that haven't even occurred! These plays don't belong in the BOX and getting ahead of yourself can result in feeling out of control.

CLEANING OUT THE BOX

Optimal performance is possible when you clear the BOX of everything except the present play. A clear BOX is quiet. There aren't a lot of thoughts clamoring for attention. A clear BOX is also clean, making it easy to find the only play that matters—*this play.* Resilience is when you clear the clutter and make the BOX a quiet and simple place for just yourself and the next play.

The resilience mechanic requires an awareness that your BOX is cluttered. The resilience mechanic also requires the ability and resources to "unstick" that clutter. Ideally, every play comes into a clean BOX so the technical and physical gears can spin freely.

Have you ever heard athletes or commentators say, "Just relax and let the game come to you"? This refers to the notion of letting a play come into the BOX, making the play, and then letting it go as the next play comes in. Instead of thinking ahead or speeding up to rectify a previous play, you slow down your thinking. You have to defend the BOX from future plays that don't belong there and sweep it clean of old plays—good, bad, or otherwise—that are no longer in your control.

Your emotions can be a helpful indicator that signal to you that a disruptive event is stuck in the BOX and needs to be cleaned out. If you're still frustrated or angry (gas on) about a bad play, or if you continue to anxiously analyze a previous mistake (gas off), it's time to do some sweeping. You can start with a deep breath and a calming self-statement like "Relax. You're good." From here you can direct your thinking back to the present—"Right now," or "Let it go"—and the current play—"This point," or "This play." As you do this, the BOX clears and quiets, you're back on cruise control, and you get locked in.

A pregame routine can help prime your resilience. To establish the proper mindset, keep your thoughts positive, present, and process-oriented. If resilience is a mental mechanic you need to work on, use some affirmations like "Nothing knocks me off my game!" or "Impossible to rattle!" This kind of self-talk strengthens your resilience. Remind yourself of the connection between resilience and performance by thinking something like *The only person who can beat me is me.* Prepare yourself for the inevitability of disruptive events—"If something goes wrong, take a breath and clear the BOX." Make sure your sports credo addresses how you want to handle setbacks and remind yourself of this before you compete. When the game or match begins, this preparation will have you in a much better place mentally to stay in the BOX and roll with anything that comes your way.

You can train your resilience for game situations by developing verbal and behavioral cues to help you stay in the BOX when something goes wrong. With practice, these cues will signal the brain to respond just the way you want it to—the calm execution of whatever the next play requires. A verbal cue is something you say to yourself that reminds and directs you to do what you need to do after a disruptive event. You might say something like "Let it go," or "Next play." To learn more about performance affirmations, see Worksheet #4 ("Say It, Believe It, Be It!") in Chapter 7.

A behavioral cue is something you do that helps you move past a bad play or call that didn't go your way. A tennis player may hit the strings of their racket three times as they say "Let-it-go." A golfer may "fix" the poor shot they just hit with a second swing. Evan Longoria, a three-time MLB All-Star, uses a behavioral cue to move past potentially disruptive events when he's batting. If he let a perfect pitch go or felt squeezed by the umpire, he steps out of the batter's box, looks at the left field foul pole, takes a deep breath, and imagines blowing the frustration right over it. That pitch is gone, and as he steps back into the batter's box, he is also stepping back into a clean BOX.

TRIGGERS AND MORE BOX HOUSEKEEPING

Learn your triggers. What kind of events have, in the past, stuck in your BOX? When you are aware of those—and it helps to be specific—you can make a conscious effort to make sure those are swept up, swept out, and tossed in the waste bin. A good exercise is to scout yourself. What are the things that upset you or that you struggle with that might stick in the BOX? Mistakes, lack of success, disappointments, or anything that doesn't go your way might be sticking with you and impacting your performance in the future.

If you know that mistakes such as errors or turnovers trigger an unwanted response, develop a new, more effective response for those situations and practice that response until it becomes automatic. For example, if you commit an error, you might train yourself to respond by pounding your glove to let the frustration out, taking a deep breath, and using an affirmation like "You're good" to get settled. Direct yourself back to the present and into the BOX, and say something like "Let's get a double play!" If missing shots is a trigger, don't dwell on the misses or open the door to doubts. Every athlete misses shots. The more productive response is to stay in the moment, play your game, and trust your abilities. If you do this, your shots will fall.

Even exchanges between you and an opponent can linger where they don't belong. Have you ever had someone on the other team "get in your head"? If so, you can recognize that situation as one of your triggers and practice responding more effectively.

One of my hockey teammates spent way too much time in the penalty box because he let opponents get to him. He thought he wasn't being tough if he didn't react aggressively. The coach wanted him on the ice and not in the penalty box, so he made a suggestion: "Laugh at them," the coach said. "Trust me; it will drive them crazy." The next time an opponent tried to bait him, my friend tried this. He laughed at the guy, who got frustrated and skated off. It worked! Laughing at anyone trying to get under his skin became a resilience tool he was able to pull out as his go-to response. As a result, he spent more time on the ice and accumulated more goals than penalty minutes.

Another common trigger for athletes is getting a bad call from an umpire or official. Bad calls are not unusual, but complaining or showing your displeasure can be costly in two ways. Complaining is a gas-on response, and as we discussed in Chapter 3, that can knock you out of the

BOX and hurt your performance. A pitcher who remains hot after a bad call is distracted from the next pitch—the only pitch they have any control over. If the pitch she's throwing isn't getting her full attention, there's a good chance the outcome won't be good.

Another problem with allowing a bad call to anger you is the reaction you risk from the official. Umpires and referees are people, too; if they feel they have been disrespected or shown up by your evident displeasure, it's likely they'll watch you more closely for an opportunity to respond.

So instead of complaining about a call that doesn't go your way, condition yourself to take a deep breath and walk away. Train your response and get out of there. Remind yourself to control the controllable and not let an official pull you out of the BOX and take you away from doing what you are capable of doing.

The idea of controlling the controllables is also applicable to conditions. No one wants to run in freezing weather, but what are you going to do about it? If you focus on how miserable you feel, you let it into the BOX, and you're distracted by negative thoughts or feelings of dread. Instead, make a mental decision that you love freezing conditions. Say to yourself, "I love running in this stuff. The cold is energizing." The affirmation keeps you from dwelling on the cold and creating negative energy and may give you an added mental edge over your opponent. You can't control the weather, so you dismiss it by putting a positive frame around it. There's no negativity when you say, "Let's just enjoy the ride," and attack the challenge. You escort the problem right out of the BOX. Now you're just running.

In the Mental Toolbox section of the book, Worksheet #5 ("Personal Game Plan") will help you scout yourself, identify your tendencies, and create a game plan for dealing with them.

REFOCUSING COMMANDS

Refocusing commands help you keep bad breaks from ever getting into the BOX (and save you the time it takes to sweep them out). As soon as something happens, you can use a refocusing command to counteract it. No break in play is required. The key is to work on these commands so that they become your language and your response is automatic. It's the best tool for the heat of battle.

For example, say you're a point guard and your job is to attack the rim and either lay it in or dump it off to a teammate if you're defended. On one play, you drive for the hoop and drop it off to your center, but you are then hammered and flung out of bounds by the defender. No call. Your center misses an easy layin, and the other team grabs the rebound and races off.

A lot of players might be slow to get to their feet, stung by the indignity and unfairness of it all. They'd raise their palms in disbelief. They'd look at their bench for affirmation that they've been mistreated. They'd hobble down the court to demonstrate just how abused and victimized they feel.

But that's not you. You're not going to let all that emotion into your BOX. You spring to your feet and shout "Get back!" which is your reminder to yourself to get back on defense. You fly down the court.

The "Get back!" exhortation is an example of a refocusing command. It's your way of blocking any distracting emotions from polluting your BOX. You are immediately back in the play.

To be effective, refocusing commands must have three ingredients.

First, they must be *immediate*. You can't wait until you've been out of the BOX for even a minute or two to then think about doing something. Too much happens in that time. As soon as the disruption occurs, you immediately use the command—before you even register being out of the BOX.

Second, the command must be *intense*. The intensity of the command is meant to be jarring and kick you back into the BOX where you belong. It's intended to jolt you out of the mindless contemplation of thinking about a bad play to the distraction of the action happening in real time.

Finally, the command has to be *instructive*. The immediacy and intensity of the self-talk gets your attention, and the instruction tells you precisely what to do next. This is not encouragement. This isn't the time for saying, "Hey, you're okay. Don't worry about it." Instead, it's a simple and direct command, such as "get back" or "next play." It tells you what to do. Get back on defense and get connected to the next play.

In the Mental Toolbox section of the book, Worksheet #7 ("Refocusing Commands") will help you develop a refocusing command that works for you.

TIME FOR THE FIVE R'S

Another resilience tool that helps you efficiently overcome a bad play is called the Five R's. Working through the Five R's takes a little more time, but can be used quickly when there's a break in the action, such as between points or after a whistle. If you are in the heat of the battle and need to get immediately back in the action, use a refocusing command. But if you have more time, run through the Five R's.

The first step is to *release* the emotion. If you are a competitive athlete, you aren't human if you don't find disruptive events upsetting. If you're not upset, you probably don't care, and that's a whole different problem. To move forward, you have to release your frustration or anger and get it out of the way.

Ideally, there is a physicality to the release. If you observe other athletes with this in mind, you may notice players pulling hard on their chin straps, whipping the Velcro on their glove, or forcefully spitting some water. These are quick responses to relieve the distracting internal pressure that intense emotion can create.

The second R is *regroup*. You've released your anger, and now it's time to regroup. Regrouping is the transition between the momentary release and getting to the point where you can be rational and figure out what happened. Taking a deep breath and saying something to yourself like "Okay, that's enough" can be all it takes.

The next step is critical and involves a *review*. This is where you think about what happened logically and analytically. Emotion cannot be a part of this step. The brain merely wants to understand and adjust, not judge or critique.

The fourth "R" is for getting back to a *relaxed* state. Take a deep breath and exhale slowly. As you exhale, use confident and calming self-talk, like "You're good!" or "You've got this!" Repeat as needed.

The final "R" is for *refocus*. At this point, you've returned to the BOX. The last play is history and you've learned from it. You're reconnected to the moment and ready. Next play!

Imagine a quarterback who has just thrown an interception. As he walks off the field, he yanks on his chin strap as a release. To regroup, he says to himself, "Alright. Enough of that." Before he gets to the sidelines, he reviews the play in his head and says, "I've got to read the safety." At that point, he has identified what happened and why he threw the interception. By the time he gets to the bench, he takes a deep breath (relaxes), grabs a Gatorade, and is mentally ready to go back into the game. He is refocused. He's back in the BOX.

In the Mental Toolbox section of the book, I've included a worksheet (Worksheet #8: "Resilience Technique") that gives a quick rundown of the Five R's and how to use them.

STACEY'S RESILIENCE TOOLKIT

Every serious golfer has a pre-shot routine that helps with consistency. They tap the club on the ground, pick their spot, and take a practice swing to help them settle in. The brain likes the routine, and it helps the shot.

Stacey found that she also needed a post-shot routine. Every shot had to be put away the same so the next shot could come into the BOX and not be affected by what had happened before. After good shots, even decent shots, Stacey was all systems go. She'd store her club and move to the next shot. When Stacey hit a bad shot, however, she reacted differently. This caused the brain to respond anxiously, which made it difficult for her to get past her mistake. By creating a post-shot routine she could implement every time, it became less likely Stacey would allow an unfortunate reaction to take her out of her best game.

Stacey adapted the Five R's strategy to help her be more resilient. If she hit a good shot, she would acknowledge it by saying, "Good shot," or "That's right where I want to be." She'd take a breath and put the club away to signal the shot was over, and she would walk to the next shot with the same tempo and energy every time. If she made a bad shot, she would squeeze the grip of her club as hard as she could and use a release statement to purge the shot—something visceral, like "Grrrrr." Releasing her grip on the club was an indication to herself that it was out of her system and she would move to the review. Once she identified what had happened, she would fix it with a practice swing. Then she would take a deep breath to relax, and as she put the club away, she'd say, "Let's go hit a great shot."

The process was the same regardless of the shot she hit; she merely added a release, regroup, and review after a bad shot. The post-shot routine developed into a process to consistently end a shot, just as her pre-shot routine consistently began her play.

Using or adapting the Five R's to your own game as Stacey did can be an effective and efficient way to refocus during play.

By working on mental mechanics, you are learning to use your thoughts to direct your actions. The more you do it, the more automatic and effective it becomes. The next chapter, on drive, also emphasizes how thinking can affect athletic performance. Once you understand the power of what's in your head, you can intentionally choose to direct your thoughts in ways that make you a better athlete.

CHAPTER 6

. . . . .

DRIVE

Success does not come from spontaneous combustion. Sometimes you have to set yourself on fire.

—ARNOLD GLASOW

Talent is never enough. With few exceptions, the best players are the hardest workers.

—MAGIC JOHNSON

Heather was a fourteen-year-old freshman who wanted to play for her high school softball team. She was involved in various clubs and played in the marching band but also wanted to play a sport as part of her high school experience. She felt softball was the best sport for her to focus on.

Unlike many of the girls who tried out for the team, Heather didn't have an extensive sports background. She had played soccer and softball at the recreational level but rarely worked on her skills in the off-season. She was a fast runner and had practiced hitting at the local batting cages, and she had hoped this would be enough to make the team.

Unfortunately, it wasn't. She was disappointed that she hadn't made the team but still had a strong desire to play and a willingness to put in the work to make that happen. As a result, Heather and her parents scheduled a consultation to explore how developing the mental game can improve performance.

It was clear that Heather wanted to make the softball team very badly. What Heather lacked was an understanding of how to channel and steer that desire to get the results she wanted. She was willing to work hard, but she also needed to learn how to work smart so she could maximize the results she got from her efforts. She needed to learn about drive.

THE ROLE OF DRIVE IN YOUR MENTAL GAME

What is drive? At its most basic level, drive is how athletes get better. Think of it as the blood, sweat, and tears gear, or the work you do away from the heat of competition. If you apply the drive mechanic well, you can reach your full potential, play better, and enjoy yourself more.

While the other mental mechanics we've discussed are about playing well when the game starts, drive is about preparing for competition in the days, weeks, and months leading up to those moments. Drive is the work you do when no one is watching. Drive is found in empty gyms, driveways, and neighborhood baseball diamonds. Drive is what gets you up at four thirty in the morning to go to swim practice or what sends you to the playground at night to shoot five hundred foul shots by the light of a streetlamp.

Drive is working with purpose. When you have drive, you are intentional about your efforts, goals, and motivations because you want to improve as an athlete. Drive is what allows you to put the emotion, mindset, confidence, and resilience to work when it's time to step into the BOX.

Drive is like desire, only greater. Desire is central to being an athlete—you must have the desire to get better—but drive channels that desire and ensures all your work and preparation is done with purpose and clear intent.

Drive is also the only mental mechanic that is future oriented. Confidence, mindset, emotions, and resilience are about playing in the BOX, but the drive mechanic prepares you to take advantage of those moments in the BOX. With a well-developed drive mechanic, you will thrive when you are in a game and do all the great things you know you are capable of doing.

Drive is about working hard, but it's more about working smart. One athlete goes to the gym for thirty minutes with a plan of action. It's an even day, so it's upper body—small muscle groups first, then large muscle groups, two sets. The other athlete goes to the gym for an hour and just works out using whatever equipment is available. Who gets better? I'll take the athlete with the plan every time.

Consider two athletes who both want to play in college. One says she has to work very hard and the other uses goal setting to create a plan to stay on track and work on specific skills where she is lacking. Both are working hard but only the latter is working smart.

It can be frustrating for athletes to work extremely hard but not make the progress they wanted. What can make the difference is drive—utilizing the mental gear to maximize gains made in the technical and physical areas. Drive provides direction (goals), sustains effort (motivation), and creates a training mindset that goes beyond simply working hard. Drive applies direct force on your physical and technical gears, strengthening and polishing them so they can spin with vigor and purpose. While desire might make you spin those gears faster and harder as you work out or practice, drive is what built them in the first place.

Drive is relevant to all aspects of life. To get where you

want to be, you must work with purpose and clear inten-
tion about what you want to accomplish.

THE ELEMENTS OF DRIVE

Drive comprises three components:

1. Goal setting
2. Motivation
3. Training approach

GOAL SETTING

Goal setting begins with your destination or *outcome goal*.
What outcome are you seeking? Once you know where
you want to go, you have to figure out how you are going
to get there.

A goal that sits in isolation is no different than a wish.
Stating a goal doesn't make it happen, any more than rub-
bing a bottle or crossing your fingers will make it happen.
Your goal may be a final destination, but to reach it you
must set different types of goals to create a path to get
you there.

Say you are a sophomore high school basketball player,
and you want to start on the varsity team next year. That's
what you want to accomplish. That's your *outcome goal*.

Now you need *focus goals* that identify what you need to do or work on to reach that goal. In this case, you must get stronger and faster and develop a better outside shot. You also need to improve your ball-handling skills.

Next you need *process goals*. This next level of goals pinpoints how you will meet your focus goals. How will you get stronger? How will you improve your speed? How will you work on your outside shot? Will you work with a personal trainer or skills coach? Will you follow an existing workout plan or create your own? Good process goals must also consider how you will implement your plan as a busy student-athlete. The pursuit of important goals requires setting priorities, time management, and personal sacrifice.

At this point, you have the makings of a plan. You know what you want, and you understand what you have to do to get there. Now you have to mark your progress with *tracking goals* that keep you focused by recording and charting the work you do and the progress you make. Tracking goals keep you accountable and signal when you might need to make adjustments. Many athletes do this by keeping a training journal or a calendar showing workouts scheduled and completed.

All these goals strung together create a map to your destination. It's no longer a wish; it's a plan.

Once your goals are in place the road toward becoming a varsity starter is more concrete. Now you must figure out how to accomplish those focus goals. To get stronger, you decide to work out five days a week and follow an online nutritional plan to add healthy weight. You are going to spend a minimum of five hours a week working on your shooting at the rec center. You commit to shooting one hundred free throws at the end of every shooting workout. Finally, you will practice dribbling for a minimum of five hours per week using dribbling drills you found on YouTube. This gives you ten hours of practice and training a week that you must fit into your schedule.

Benchmarks will also keep you on track, so you set intermittent goals. You intend to gain ten pounds by August 1st and increase your bench press and squat by 20 percent by the time camp starts. You also want to be able to make 70 percent of your free throws by August 1st and increase your speed on dribbling drills by five seconds. Specific goals with time frames help with focus and motivation.

MOTIVATION

Motivation is the feeling component to goal setting. It's the emotional response to important goals. If goals are your map to get where you're going, motivation is the fuel.

Different people need different fuel, so it helps to know

yourself. If you have an internal focus, you are motivated by a desire to have fun, be the best, or reach your full potential. Motivation tends to push you from the inside rather than pull you from the outside. Winning a trophy may not fuel you as much as achieving a personal best. Hope Solo, a US soccer goalkeeper and two-time Olympic gold medalist, describes her intrinsic motivation this way: "People don't put pressure on me. I just play for the love of the game."

Externally motived athletes are on the other end of the spectrum. Golfer Arnold Palmer was one. Palmer once said, "Winning isn't everything, but wanting it is." If you are like Palmer, you are driven by things like honors, scholarships, and winning championships.

Think about yourself. What's the fuel for your competitive engine?

THE STAGES OF MOTIVATION

There are two stages of motivation.

The first stage is the desire, or starting the fire. At the beginning, motivation is generally red hot.

However, the road to big goals is usually long, and uphill in places, which brings us to the second stage: sustaining motivation. How do you remain motivated and keep stoking the fire so it continues burning?

Staying motivated is a challenge for every athlete. It helps to surround yourself with regular inspiration. Many athletes use quotes for this. A hockey player might put this quote from Wayne Gretzky in a prominent location: "The highest compliment that you can pay me is to say that I work hard every day, that I never dog it." A soccer player might have this from Mia Hamm: "I am building a fire, and every day I train I add more fuel. At just the right moment, I light the match." My personal favorite quote comes from Hall of Fame wide receiver Jerry Rice, who said, "Today I'll do what others won't so that tomorrow I can do what others can't."

Music has a powerful effect on human emotion and can be a great motivational tool. That's why you see so many athletes wearing headphones. Put together personal playlists that deliver fuel you can burn for energy during a tough workout. Watch YouTube videos and follow athletes you admire on social media for inspiration.

WHAT'S IN THE PROS' HEADPHONES?

Athlete	Listens To
LeBron James	Hip-hop and rap
Michelle Wie	Reggae and rap
Cristiano Ronaldo	Pop and Brazilian
Gabby Douglass	Hip-hop and gospel
Derek Jeter	R&B and hip-hop
Peyton Manning	Country and rock
Danica Patrick	Rock and R&B
Usain Bolt	Pop and reggae
Serena Williams	Pop and Hip Hop
Michael Phelps	Hip-hop and rap

When the flame starts to fade, reconnect to your outcome goal, or destination, and remind yourself why you're working so hard. Remember why it's worth it. Put up a photo of the university you want to play for in your room or occasionally remind yourself with verbal cues like "This is how you become a starter." All of these tips can help you tap into a reserve of fuel you didn't know you had.

A training partner who pushes you and keeps you accountable is another way to stay motivated. A like-minded athlete with a similar mindset can keep you working hard even when your tank is low.

Don't be surprised when you struggle to keep the fire blazing. There will be setbacks. However, setbacks and failures can make you physically stronger and mentally tougher. Smooth seas make bad sailors. When the day's training has been frustrating, don't let it discourage you. Think of it as the gritty part of your journey, a reminder that what you're attempting is not easy. Big goals are never easy. Tough days make you stronger. Put the day away and refuel for tomorrow.

TRAINING APPROACH

The third critical component of drive has to do with how you approach practice and training. Hall of Fame football coach Vince Lombardi famously said, "Practice doesn't make perfect. Perfect practice makes perfect." All athletes train their bodies and practice their skills, but those who understand the drive mechanic know that *how* they train and practice can be the difference between being good and being great.

The drive mechanic emphasizes being intentional when training and practicing. Being intentional means not merely going through the motions, but knowing why you are doing something and how you want to do it. Most serious athletes train hard and give strong efforts in practice. However, many times these efforts can be undermined by a mindset that suggests practice or training are chores to get over with. Athletes with this mindset tend to take a passive approach—be on time, do what the coach tells you to do, and get out of there. A well-developed drive mechanic helps athletes engage more fully in practice and training sessions and get more out of them.

The drive mechanic emphasizes being intentional in three areas: **purpose**, **focus**, and **execution**.

Purpose means you make sure every practice or training session is connected to something meaningful. People work harder and make greater sacrifices for things that are important to them. The athlete that looks at practice as the place to earn a starting job, or to prepare for success on Friday night under the lights will practice with a greater sense of purpose than a teammate who thinks of it simply as practice.

Focus means you have a plan for every practice or workout. All athletes should be attentive during drills or when the coach is going over game plans, but the focus we're talking about goes beyond those behaviors. This focus emphasizes the specifics of what you will work on and what you need to improve on. Even before taking the floor or the field, you need to determine your objectives for the upcoming session. For example, a volleyball player preparing for practice might say, "I have to work on my hitting. I need to make sure my footwork is right and use my arms to elevate." When practice begins, she'll be primed to improve this important skill.

Execution is an essential area of drive because it emphasizes technical perfection and being deliberate in your approach. Poor mechanics and sloppy execution in practice can lead to poor mechanics and sloppy execution in games. Practicing good mechanics and crisp execution helps ensure those qualities become automatic when they matter the most. Practicing deliberately means committing yourself to being locked in when you're working on a skill or drill and making sure you're doing it the right way. You can also be deliberate about your effort and attitude. Bring intensity, energy, and positivity to every practice; in addition to making you a better athlete, this will set a tone for practice that makes your team better.

Nothing builds confidence more than knowing that you work as hard as, or harder than, anyone you'll compete against. Athletes who master the drive mechanic gain confidence knowing they don't just work hard, they work smart. This kind of confidence enhances every other mental mechanic and ensures that all three gears are good to go. That's a complete athlete.

HEATHER'S DRIVE

Heather may not have been the best athlete at her high school, but she was motivated and held tight to her goal of making the softball team her sophomore year. All she needed was a road map that identified what she needed to work on, directed her efforts, and helped her stay on track as she pursued her goal. In other words, she had to work through the drive mechanic.

First, she identified specific areas of her game that she felt she needed to improve: batting, fielding, and overall fitness. These became her focus goals. Her process goals easily fell into place. She committed to practicing hitting in the basement and working on fielding five days a week. She worked with a physical trainer once a week to improve her strength and flexibility and worked out on her own another three times per week. Finally, she worked with a professional instructor to improve her technical skills.

Heather had a clear purpose. She was determined to become a complete athlete and make the softball team, and this created an intentional approach to her practice and training sessions. She began every session by identifying what she was going to work on and why working hard was important to her. She was committed to pushing herself as hard as she could to become stronger and more fit. She emphasized deliberate practice to build strong and reliable mechanics. She used a large desktop calendar to organize her training and make sure she was staying on track.

To keep her motivation strong, Heather took a picture

of the team roster, pinned it to the bulletin board in her room, and wrote, "Someone is missing" on it. She placed positive affirmations such as "Hard work gets you there," "Better every day," and "You've got this" in strategic locations around her house and repeated them throughout her day. She also began following athletes she respected on social media for motivation and inspiration.

Heather's hard work and intentional efforts paid off. She made the team!

YOU CAN BE A COMPLETE ATHLETE

Congratulations on making it to this point in the book. By now, you know that working on your mental gear is as important as your technical and physical training. All three gears have to turn freely if you want to be the best athlete you can be.

It's not a flaw or personal weakness to have an underdeveloped mental gear. But you do have to recognize that weak gear because it's impossible to work on something that you don't understand. Being told not to let something "get in your head" or to work on your "mental toughness" doesn't help you understand or give you any direction.

All athletes benefit from strengthening their mental gear so it can turn in concert with their physical and technical gears. Your mental gear must become another facet of your training. The mechanics of the mental game—managing your confidence, directing your thinking, regulating your emotions, handling disruptions, and maximizing your training through drive—must be practiced just as you practice your passing, shooting, and hitting skills.

Now that you understand the importance of your mental game, how it works, and how it can help you, it's time for you to get to work. The next chapter provides tools and exercises that will help you develop your overall mental game and address specific challenges you may experience. Approach them in the same way you might approach a workout or your technical training. The result of working at all three gears is optimal performance from a complete athlete.

CHAPTER 7

. . . . .

THE MENTAL TOOLBOX

The following pages contain a number of worksheets, concepts, and exercises that will help you develop your mental gear. Consider these your training documents. Review them and do the exercises from time to time to ensure that you are developing a mental gear to match your physical and technical gears.

When I work with athletes, I include many of these worksheets in the athletes' performance plans. Some of the exercises are conceptual, but others will require that you put pencil to paper. The writing exercises in particular make your thoughts concrete and raise them to a new level of importance. This is vital if you really want to develop that mental gear.

Reading and completing these exercises enables you to realize that things like confidence are less a fleeting sensation and more of an actual skill that you can nurture, strengthen, and incorporate purposefully with your thinking and actions. They also help you become aware of your self-talk and adjust that self-talk in a way that keeps negative, performance-hindering thoughts out of the BOX.

All of these exercises are helpful, but you can also pick and choose the ones that seem most valuable to you. Each exercise has a training note at the bottom describing which mental mechanic that particular exercise was designed for. If, for example, you feel you mostly need help with developing resilience, you can go directly to the worksheets that address that aspect of your mental game.

Even as you master these mental mechanics, it pays to return to them from time to time. They can help you fine-tune your mental gear or get back on track if you're struggling. Commit to your mental game just like you commit to your physical and technical training. You may work your way through the Toolbox differently as your game evolves and your goals change. For example, your sense of identity may change over the course of a couple years. You might grow from a six-foot freshman weighing 140 pounds who just wants to make the high school team to a six-five, 215-pound junior who has his sights set on playing in college.

Fine-tuning your mental gear as you mature athletically is the same as making physical and technical adjustments as you grow and gain more skills. Just as your shot or your swing is likely to change as you get bigger and stronger, your mental game will, too, requiring adjustments to your mental gear. Circling back and going over these tools in the Mental Toolbox can help you with that.

You may find it useful to hang on to your old worksheets and review them. It's never a bad thing to go back and look at what you wrote when you were fourteen. Sometimes, it can make you realize *Wow, I've really grown!* Looking back at old worksheets can also prompt you to reflect on the person you have become. I've had many athletes take their performance plan to college with them. They might feel like the mental gear is a little stuck, so they go through the worksheets and summaries and it helps them rediscover the techniques that helped them in the past. They rediscover strong mental mechanics.

You'll also find a lot of overlap in the items in the Mental Toolbox. For example, your work on confidence will also help your resilience. If you're improving your confidence, you're also likely improving your ability to recover from disruptive events. These mental mechanics are all closely related, so expect to improve in more than one area as you work through the following pages.

If you want to download and print out copies of the following worksheets, you can find them on my website, www.mindseyesports.com.

WORSHEET #1

. . . . .

SELF-AWARENESS

IDENTITY, JOB, APPROACH

Athletes who know who they are athletically (identity), what they need to do to be successful (job), and how they need to do it (approach) are more confident, experience less pre-performance nerves, and consistently perform at or near the peak of their abilities.

Identity: What skills and abilities make you the athlete that you are? It is important to know this so that you can be confident in your abilities and play to your strengths. Example: *I'm very fast, I see the field well, and I do a good job of getting the ball to my teammates when they're open.*

Job: What are the most important things you need to do when you play to perform the way you want to and help your team? Knowing what you need to do to be successful helps confidence and keeps you focused on your process—what you need to *do* to play your best. Example: *I need to play with high energy, be physical under the basket, and look to score when I'm open.*

Approach: How do you need to play to be at your best? What do you look like when you're playing great? Should you be intense and locked in or loose and playful? Should your energy be frenetic or restrained? Would you be smiling or very serious? Every athlete has their own approach to playing their sport, and they need to stay true to it to play their best. Example*: I need to have fun, fly around and take chances, and talk to my teammates.*

For the self-aware athlete, establishing the right mindset before a game is as easy as thinking, *All I need to do is go out there and be me, do my job, and do it my way.* This can also help when you're struggling. For example, at halftime you can tell yourself, *I just need to get back to being me, doing my job, and playing the way I play.*

SELF-AWARENESS WORKSHEET

Identity: Think about what makes you the athlete you are. What are your strongest natural abilities? Are you physically strong? Fast? Agile? Do you have great stamina? Intensity? What are your strongest skills? Do you shoot well? Putt well? Pass well? Do you have good vision? The ability to anticipate plays? Write your top three strengths below.

Job: Think about what you need to do to play your best and help your team. You will do many things during the course of a game or match, but what is the most important for you to play well? Do you have to play tough defense? Look to score? Set up your teammates? Keep in mind that jobs are processes, not outcomes. For example, a job could be to be aggressive at the plate, not get a hit. Write the three most important things you need to do below.

Approach: Think about the best game you've ever played. How were you playing? What did it look like? Were you loose and freewheeling or methodical and patient? Were you animated or serious? Talking or quiet? In the space below, describe what you look like when you're playing your best.

Now, when you need to get into a good mindset before playing, it's as simple as saying, *Be you, do your job, do it your way*!

CONFIDENCE EQUATION

THINK LIKE A CHAMPION

Remember, the Confidence Equation is confident thinking + confident behavior = confident feeling. *Self-talk* is the inner dialogue all athletes engage in. As the name implies, it's how we talk to ourselves. And that "how" is *critical*. Why? Because our thinking, or self-talk, impacts our emotions and the execution of our skills. It's the first half of the Confidence Equation.

THE DOUBTER VERSUS THE BELIEVER

Imagine that you have two athletes living in your head. Let's call one the "Doubter." The Doubter's tone of voice is negative. "Don't mess up!" this athlete says. The Doubter is also anxious and focused on what they hope won't happen. "I hope we don't lose," the Doubter says. "I hope I don't play badly." This self-talk creates pressure and anxiousness, and it can lead to tentative play and poor performance.

Let's call the other athlete the "Believer." The Believer's tone of voice is positive. "I'm ready!" this athlete says. The Believer is also confident and focused on what they plan on doing. "I'm going to play great!" the Believer says. "I'm going to give everything I've got!" This athlete is focused on process, or the "job." "Play with energy!" is the Believer's message. "Be aggressive!" "Have fun."

These two athletes—the Doubter and the Believer—feed on your thoughts. The one you feed the most is the one who takes the field or steps onto the court. To think like a champion, you have to develop your self-talk. You can do this by creating self-talk scripts for key times and situations that will protect, if not enhance, your confidence. With practice, your new responses will become automatic and you will be hard to knock out of the BOX.

SELF-TALK WORKSHEET: THINKING
LIKE A CHAMPION

You can't leave your self-talk to chance. You can't simply wait and see where it takes you. It's too important to your confidence and the way you will step onto the field or court. You must train yourself to have the right thoughts at the right time.

A great way to do this is to script your ideal self-talk for key times and situations. Think about how you want to be talking to yourself in the situations below. Keep the elements of confident thinking in mind and make sure your self-talk is positive (sounds like an encouraging coach or teammate) and focused on process (the things you *do* to get the outcome you want). Write down your two strongest statements.

On your way to a game or match:

1.

2.

When you arrive:

1.

2.

Warming up:

1.

2.

When the game or match is starting:

1.

2.

After a setback:

1.

2.

You have just identified the thinking half of your Confidence Equation. You know how you need to be thinking from the time you leave for a game or match until it is over. Commit these thoughts to memory and consistently use them in these situations. The Doubter may still try to make some noise once in a while but, in time, your positive self-talk will become automatic and the Believer will be the only voice you hear. You'll be thinking like a champion.

Training Note: Helpful with the following Mental Mechanics: Confidence, Mindset, Emotions, Resilience, Drive

CONFIDENCE EQUATION

ACT LIKE A CHAMPION

Remember, the Confidence Equation is confident thinking + confident behavior = confident feeling. Our brains interpret and respond to what we *do*. Our body language, the way we react to adversity, and even the tempo and energy we play with all send signals to the brain that it quickly analyzes to create a response (how we feel and what we do). Some behaviors will create the response you want—sustained confidence and business-as-usual play. Some will create a response no one wants—diminished confidence, distracting emotions, and a fading performance.

Athletes need to know what behaviors help them to consistently get into the BOX, stay in the BOX, and play in the BOX. For example, a golfer walks at a brisk pace between shots and enjoys interacting with her fellow competitors. This is her confident behavior, and her brain knows it. However, when she's not playing well, her pace slows and she becomes quiet. This change in behavior sends a different message to the brain, and the response has a negative impact on her confidence and play. Acting like a champion means engaging in your confident behaviors at all times, especially if you're struggling.

What are your confident behaviors? To master the behavior part of the Confidence Equation, athletes must understand the connection between their actions, responses, and performance. They must know what works best for them—their own style and approach. Some athletes need to be smiling and interacting with teammates. Some need to be more "locked in." Some athletes need to play with a lot of energy and at a quick tempo. Some need to be more deliberate and methodical.

Knowing your style of play enables you to train yourself to be consistent with your body language, reactions to setbacks, tempo, and energy. This in turn will send positive signals to the brain that help you consistently play your best.

CONFIDENT BEHAVIOR WORKSHEET:
ACTING LIKE A CHAMPION

Think about one of your best performances as an athlete. Take some time to remember it clearly and in as much detail as possible. Describe what this would have looked like to someone observing you at the times listed below.

An hour before the game/match:

In the locker room:

Warming up:

While playing:

After a setback:

You just described the behavior part of your Confidence Equation in greater detail. This is what you look like and what you do when you're playing your best. These behaviors trigger the confident response you want. This is what you should look like *all the time*, regardless of how things seem to be going. When you do, you'll be acting like a champion.

Training Note: Helpful with the following Mental Mechanics: Confidence, Mindset, Emotion, Resilience, Drive

. . . . .

SAY IT, BELIEVE IT, BE IT!

PERFORMANCE AFFIRMATIONS

Performance affirmations are strong, positive statements spoken out loud or in your head throughout your day. They can have a powerful impact on your conscious and unconscious thinking. Affirmations can develop qualities you want to see in yourself as an athlete, as well as in your performance. The science of affirmations is pretty simple: repetition builds belief. The more you say something and hear something, the more the brain believes it to be true. When these statements are positive—*I will, I can, I do*—the beliefs they create provide high-octane fuel for your confidence.

Performance affirmations are stated as truths, not wishes. They are grounded in the present, not the future. They are

"I am," not "I will be." They are "I will," not "I hope." If you want to handle pressure situations better, your performance affirmation would be "Pressure brings out the best in me!" not "I will get better at handling pressure."

Performance affirmations train your brain throughout your day and week to think like a champion. Well-established affirmations are a strong defense against negative thinking, which can chip away at confidence and deplete motivation. When it's time to compete, your affirmations become powerful mantras that help you get into the BOX, stay in the BOX, and play in the BOX.

SAMPLE PERFORMANCE AFFIRMATIONS:

- I make plays!
- I love big moments!
- Pressure makes me a beast!
- I'm in control!
- Nothing rattles me!
- I can beat anyone!
- Calm, focused, ready!
- I never quit!
- Mentally tough, physically strong!
- I love this game!
- Stronger as others weaken!
- I trust my game!
- I play in the BOX!

SAY IT, BELIEVE IT, BE IT!
BUILDING YOUR OWN PERFORMANCE
AFFIRMATIONS

Think about a quality you want to develop or strengthen related to *yourself* as an athlete (e.g., work ethic, resilience, confidence, etc.). Select affirmations from the list of examples or create some yourself that will help you develop that quality. Write them below.

Now, think about an aspect of *your performance* that you want to develop or strengthen (e.g., handling pressure situations, trusting your game, being more aggressive, etc.). Select affirmations from the list of examples or create some yourself that will help you develop that quality. Write them below.

Commit to these affirmations to develop and strengthen the qualities you desire. Write them down and put them where you will see them on a regular basis—in your room, on the bathroom mirror, in your locker. Say them out loud or in your head, boldly and with conviction, throughout your day, remembering that repetition builds belief and belief fuels confidence.

Training Note: Helpful with the following Mental Mechanics: Confidence, Mindset, Emotions, Resilience, Drive

WORSHEET #5

. . . . .

PERSONAL GAME PLAN

DON'T BEAT YOURSELF

Why do coaches scout their opponents? It's simple. If a coach knows an opposing team's tendencies—what they do a high percentage of the time—the coach can create a game plan incorporating strategic responses to these tendencies. For example: "When they're in this formation, we will do this." "When this player is in the game, this is the defense we will run."

For many athletes, their thoughts and reactions to disruptive events (bad plays, bad breaks, or distractions) become inner opponents that make it difficult for them to play well. They may react to a bad play with a thought that undermines their confidence (*I stink!*). They may compromise their focus by dwelling on things they can't control (*This ump is awful!*). Or they may produce excessive anxiety and pressure by thinking about outcomes (*What if I don't play well?*). It's difficult enough to play against the other team; you don't want to make it any harder.

Scout yourself: Think about yourself before games and during games. What distracting events or situations tend to have a negative impact on your performance? Do you get extremely nervous before games? Do you get really upset over bad calls? Do you become tentative after mistakes? These are your inner opponents and they are detrimental to your performance. Identify your biggest inner opponent and write it in the space below.

Example: I lose confidence if I turn the ball over.

Identify your tendencies: Take your inner opponent and write down the *thoughts* that accompany it and the *responses* those thoughts trigger. These are the tendencies that can keep you from performing at the peak of your abilities. These tendencies must be countered by your personal game plan. Write your tendencies in the space below.

My tendencies *(Examples)*

Inner Opponent: *Lose confidence if I turn the ball over.*

Thoughts: *I can't handle this press. Coach is going to pull me.*

Response: *Play tentatively, look to get rid of the ball as soon as I get it.*

My tendencies

Inner Opponent: _____

Thoughts: _____

Response: _____

Create your game plan: You've scouted yourself and identified the tendencies that need to be addressed. You know
the thoughts and responses that need a new game plan.
Target your inner opponent with a simple equation: when
this happens, I will do this. For example, you might write,
"When I'm nervous before a game, I will remind myself to stay
in the present and focus on my controllables." Or "When a ref
makes a bad call, I will walk away immediately, take a deep
breath, and tell myself to let it go." Write your game plan.

Example

When <u>I turn the ball over</u>, I will <u>say, "you're good!" and sprint</u> <u>back to play defense.</u>

When _____, I will _____

The successful execution of any game plan requires commitment (belief in the plan) and effort (practice). Work at your personal game plan in practice and games. It won't work overnight, but with commitment and practice you'll conquer your inner opponents and spend more time playing in the BOX.

If you have more than one inner opponent, as most athletes do, you can download additional Personal Game Plan worksheets from the Mind's Eye Sports Performance website: www.mindseyesports.com.

Training Note: Helpful with the following Mental Mechanics: Confidence, Mindset, Emotions, Resilience

WORKSHEET #6

· · · · ·

PERFORMANCE BREATHING

THE TENSION BUSTER

Performance breathing is the application of a centuries-old breathing technique (abdominal breathing) in competitive situations to calm nerves, loosen muscles, and focus attention. As a tool, performance breathing is always available and can be used before games to help athletes get into the BOX, during games to work through a setback, or prior to the execution of a specific skill (like shooting a free throw or throwing a pitch).

After mastering this simple technique, you will find that even one breath can slow your heart rate, settle your thoughts, and keep your skills sharp. This is a tool that can help anytime you're feeling anxious and in any type of performance situation, whether it's taking a penalty kick or a calculus exam.

PERFORMANCE BREATHING TECHNIQUE

1. Place one hand on your stomach and the other on your chest. Breathe in deeply through your nose as you push your stomach out with the air you breathe in. The hand on your stomach should move; the one on your chest should not (once you have the hang of this you can stop using your hands).

2. Hold the breath until you feel a comfortable tension (aka, you feel like you would like to exhale).

3. Exhale the breath completely through your lips.

4. As you are exhaling, mentally say a cue word such as "focus" or "ready." Doing this will create a powerful connection between your breath and your cue word, making it possible to quickly relax and create the mindset you need.

5. Repeat steps 1 through 4 until you feel calmer and more relaxed. Notice the effect this also has on your thinking (clearer, more focused, etc.).

Practice this simple yet powerful tool every day (right before bed is a perfect time). This will reinforce the connection between your breath and the response you want so that, in a stressful situation, a single breath can keep you in the BOX or help you return to it.

Training Note: Helpful with the following Mental Mechanics: Confidence, Mindset, Emotions, Resilience

WORSHEET #7

· · · · ·

RESILIENCE TECHNIQUE

PROTECTING THE BOX
REFOCUSING COMMANDS

Every athlete needs to know how to immediately let go of a bad play, bad break, or distraction. Failure to do so can pull you out of the BOX and hinder performance. A refocusing command is a short, positive, and instructive word or statement used immediately after a bad play, bad break, or distraction. The refocusing command stops negative self-talk before it can begin. It keeps you in the BOX and focused on the next play. Refocusing commands have three criteria. They should be:

Immediate: They are used as soon as the distracting or upsetting event occurs.

Intense: They need to be strong and loud (in your head) to snap your focus back to the present.

Instructive: They need to provide clear direction for what you should do next.

Examples: After turning the ball over, a basketball player may immediately and strongly say, "Get back!" to focus on getting back and playing strong defense. A figure skater who falls may say, "Finish strong!" to direct their focus to the remaining elements of their routine.

Developing your own refocusing commands:

What are the negative events common to your sport? What happens that can throw you off your game? Create refocusing commands for these situations, making sure they meet all three criteria. Use them in practice and games. Before you know it, they will become automatic responses that keep you in the BOX when something bad happens.

Distracting or upsetting event:

Refocusing command:

Training Note: Helpful with the following Mental Mechanics: Confidence, Mindset, Emotions, Resilience

WORSHEET #8

• • • • •

RESILIENCE TECHNIQUE

CLEARING THE BOX
THE FIVE R'S

Refocusing after a bad play or tough break is an essential skill for all athletes because *all athletes* make bad plays and experience tough breaks. Having a *process* for handling these situations is an important tool to recover mentally when faced with adversity. The Five R's is an excellent technique to empty the BOX and get back on track.

The Five R's

Release: Get rid of the negative energy: being upset is inevitable. But do something to get the anger and frustration out. Remember that it is important to remain in control. You don't want your opponent thinking you're losing it. Pulling hard on a chinstrap, adjusting gloves, or forcefully spitting water are some examples of "releases" used by athletes. Once you've released this energy, it's time to...

Regroup: Compose yourself. After letting that intense feeling out, it is important to get yourself back together quickly, because the only play you can make is the *next play*. Take a deep breath and direct yourself to let go of the emotion. Tell yourself, "Relax. You're good!" and then...

Review: This is a critical step! The brain only wants to understand what happened so it can make the necessary adjustments. It *does not* want to judge what just happened! Think about the event in an objective, analytical, and completely unemotional manner. Figure out what happened (e.g., "I got out of position"). Tell yourself what you need to do differently next time (what you need to do to "fix it"), trust that you will make the adjustment, and...

Relax: Reconnect to the moment and surroundings. Take another deep breath. Remind yourself that you love this game and perform best when you're calm and enjoying yourself. The mistake is now history, and you've learned from it. The only play to make is the one that's in the BOX now, so it's time to...

Refocus: Step into the uncluttered BOX, focus on what you need to do, and make *this play!*

Training Note: Helpful with the following Mental Mechanics: Confidence, Mindset, Emotions, Resilience

DRIVE: GETTING WHERE YOU WANT TO GO

GOAL-SETTING WORKSHEET

This worksheet will help you with the goal-setting component of the drive mechanic. Begin by identifying a single *outcome goal*. This is what you want to accomplish. Once you've done this, follow the prompts to complete the goal-setting process for this particular goal by identifying your *focus goals*, *process goals*, and *tracking goals*. Although you should have just one *outcome goal*, you should have more than one goal for each of the *focus, process*, and *tracking* sections of your worksheet. When you're done, you will have identified what you want to accomplish as well as a detailed plan for doing it.

Outcome goal: What do you want?

Focus goals: What do you need to work on to reach your goal?

Process goals: How will you work on your focus goals?

Tracking goals: How will you know you're making progress and staying on track?

GOAL-SETTING WORKSHEET—EXAMPLE

Outcome goal:

I will make the varsity basketball team and become a starter as a junior.

Focus goals:

Improve my overall strength, improve my shooting skills, improve my dribbling skills.

Process goals:

Improve strength:

- *Work out (home or gym) five days a week.*
- *Follow a nutritional program for adding healthy weight.*

Improve shooting skills:

- *Practice shooting a minimum of five hours a week.*
- *Make one hundred free throws every shooting session.*

Improve dribbling skills:

- *Practice dribbling a minimum of five hours a week.*
- *Create a list of dribbling drills and exercises to use.*

Tracking goals:

Improve strength:

- *Gain ten pounds by August 1st.*
- *Increase bench press and squat by 20 percent by August 1st.*

Improve shooting skills:

- *Make 70 percent of my free throws by August 1st.*
- *Track my shooting workouts on my training calendar.*

Improve dribbling skills:

- *Improve my "cone drill" time by five seconds by August 1st.*
- *Track my dribbling workouts on my training calendar.*

Training Note: Helpful with the following Mental Mechanics: Confidence, Mindset, Resilience, Drive

· · · · ·

DRIVE: GETTING WHERE YOU WANT TO GO

MOTIVATION WORKSHEET

This worksheet will help you understand what motivates you and how to keep that fire burning as you pursue your next-level goals. Begin by plainly stating what you want to accomplish or your outcome goal. Then follow the prompts to clarify why this goal is important to you, identify specific things that will motivate you, and lay out strategies to keep you motivated until you reach your destination.

Outcome goal: What do you want to accomplish?

Meaning: Why is this goal important to you?

Intrinsic motivator: How will you feel when you accomplish your goal?

Extrinsic motivator: What will happen when you accomplish your goal?

Lighting the fire: How will you get motivated to pursue your goal?

Stoking the fire: How will you stay motivated when it gets tough or discouraging?

MOTIVATION WORKSHEET—EXAMPLE

What do you want (outcome goal)?

I want to earn a D-I scholarship to play softball in college.

Why is this important to you (meaningful)?

I have wanted to play in college since I was twelve. I want to become one of the best players my school has ever had and live my dream.

Describe how you will feel when you accomplish your goal (intrinsic motivators).

I will feel very proud because I worked hard and did everything I could to become the best. I will be really excited about the opportunities I'll have.

Describe what will happen when you accomplish your goal (extrinsic motivators).

I will be a D-I athlete! I will be one of the top players in the country. I will be playing on a larger stage—more attention, better facilities, and opportunities to travel with my teammates.

How will you motivate yourself to pursue your goal (lighting the fire)?

Before every workout or practice I will:

- *Listen to one of my fire-up playlists*
- *Picture myself playing for the University of Georgia*
- *Set my focus and attitude to have a great workout or practice*

How will you stay motivated when it gets tough or discouraging (stoking the fire)?

Remind myself why it's important to me, what it will feel like, and what will happen when I accomplish my goal.

Talk to my trainer, who can always make me feel better and keep me on track.

Watch some of my favorite motivational videos about grit and determination.

Training Note: Helpful with the following Mental Mechanics: Confidence, Mindset, Resilience, Drive

WORKSHEET #11

· · · · ·

INTENTIONAL PRACTICE

TAKING YOUR PRACTICE TO THE NEXT LEVEL

If athletes want to do well in their sport, they need to practice. If they want to be great, they need to practice a lot. If they want to stand out from other great athletes, they've got to practice differently. Showing up and doing what the coach tells you won't give you an edge, nor will it maximize your true potential. If you want to take your game to the next level, you've got to take your practice to the next level. This is done by being intentional in your efforts. An athlete practicing intentionally is *purposeful*, *focused*, and *deliberate*.

Purpose: When someone's work is meaningful to them, they naturally invest more into it. They are willing to make sacrifices and work harder. Connecting your practice to something important to you, such as getting more playing time, will help you dig deeper and get more out of it.

Reconnecting to your purpose during a practice can also help when your focus or effort begins to slip.

Focus: Intentional practice requires going beyond listening to the coach and paying attention during drills. You must have a specific plan for every practice or workout. Athletes practicing at the next level know exactly what they need to work on and target those areas before every practice. For example, "I really need to work on getting rid of the ball faster today." Establishing this type of focus primes their brain to take advantage of those opportunities and improve where they need to the most.

Deliberate: When you are working on your skills and plays, strive for perfect mechanics and precise execution. Experience and muscle memory make it possible for an athlete to practice without being completely focused (e.g., shooting free throws while talking to a teammate about the day's events). This can result in practicing sloppy mechanics and significantly reduce the gains an athlete makes. Athletes practicing at the next level emphasize great execution when no one is watching so they can benefit from it when everyone is watching.

If you want to play in the BOX, you have to practice in the BOX. Preparing to have a next-level practice takes less than thirty seconds. Before joining your teammates, create an intentional mindset by answering three questions:

Why does this matter?

What am I going to work on today?

How will I practice today?

Training Note: Helpful with the Following Mental Mechanics: Confidence, Mindset, Resilience, Drive

. . . . .

MENTAL IMAGERY

THE GYM THAT NEVER CLOSES

Mental imagery (visualization) is a powerful tool available to athletes anytime, anywhere. This technique can be used to practice specific skills or routines. It can also be used to visualize a major achievement or goal.

The key to productive mental imagery is to use the proper perspective and to involve as many of your senses as possible. The correct perspective is an inside-out view. Let's say you want to work on hitting out of a sand trap. With an inside-out perspective, you would see the ball in the sand and the green in front of you, as opposed to viewing yourself from the gallery.

Involving multiple senses is critical because this is how you convince your brain that you possess the skill you're imagining. Think about suspenseful movies. Multiple senses are stimulated at the theater, which makes your brain experience the movie as if it is real. This is why you feel excited or frightened. If you can create a similarly vivid "movie" of the skill you want to work on, your brain will enter that reality and respond as it would if you were physically practicing. This is a great way to get extra, perfect reps!

MENTAL IMAGERY PROCEDURE (GOLF)

1. Chose a time when you won't be interrupted and free your mind of all distractions. Use some *performance breathing* (Worksheet #6) to relax. Commit yourself to this session of mental practice.

2. Close your eyes and begin your session by seeing yourself standing confidently on the golf course. Look around and notice all the familiar sights. Hear the sounds. Feel the grass beneath your feet.

3. When you feel ready, draw your focus and attention to the specific skill you will be working on. For example, hitting out of sand traps more successfully.

4. Begin by feeling your shoes settle into the sand. Feel yourself finding the exact balance you want. See the ball with your marking lying in the sand. Tell yourself that you will

knock it close to the pin. Notice your wedge resting just above the sand, settling into the exact place you want it to. Keep your eye on the ball as you draw your club back. Feel the club begin to descend effortlessly. See and feel it make perfect contact with sand and ball, sending both toward your target. Watch your shot as it lands exactly where you want it to and rolls gently within a foot of the cup. Feel the excitement and pleasure that comes from hitting such a great shot.

5. Repeat step number four many times, making sure to execute the skill perfectly, just the way you want to, every time.

6. Open your eyes and feel the confidence and satisfaction that comes from a great practice session because that is what you just had!

Training Note: Helpful with the Following Mental Mechanics: Confidence, Mindset, Emotion, Drive

. . . . .

PERFORMANCE PLAYLISTS

MUSIC AND MINDSET

Picture Michael Phelps sitting poolside an hour before his race, or Serena Williams warming up before her match. How about Tom Brady throwing passes before gearing up, or LeBron James walking from the team bus to the locker room? Despite the fact that these champion athletes play different sports, they would all be wearing a common piece of equipment: headphones.

Studies have shown that listening to music has a variety of benefits for athletes, including regulating emotions, increasing energy, improving focus, and speeding recovery. Music stimulates multiple areas of the brain, making it a powerful part of your *mental pregame warm-up*. Carefully selected music can help you consistently get into the BOX.

PERFORMANCE PLAYLISTS

Music can move you emotionally and toward the BOX. It can energize you when you're flat, relax you when you're tense, and keep you right where you are when your mindset is good. Create three playlists that will help you get into the BOX—one to get going, one to settle yourself, and one that works when you're already there.

Energizing playlist:

Calming playlist:

Good-to-go playlist:

Training Note: Helpful with the following Mental Mechanics: Confidence, Mindset, Emotions, Resilience, Drive

WORKSHEET #14

· · · · ·

MENTAL AND EMOTIONAL STAMINA

MAINTENANCE FOR THE THIRD GEAR

The life of an athlete is a demanding balancing act. Practices, training sessions, and games require a huge commitment of time and energy. And that's only part of your life. Taking care of yourself is the key to meeting the challenges that come your way on and off the field or court.

As an athlete, you understand the importance of getting good sleep and eating well, but this neglects the third gear, the mental gear. If you want to be a *complete athlete*, you have to care for a complete athlete—*mind* and body. This requires knowing how to attend to your emotional and psychological well-being. The five tips below can help you stay emotionally strong and mentally sharp all season long.

1. **Know how to turn down the volume.** It's important to know how to settle yourself down when the pressure is on or when things get stressful (in sports and life in general). Learn how to use your breathing to calm yourself in tense moments. Become familiar with some basic meditation or mindfulness techniques for stressful times (there are some excellent apps for smartphones).

2. **Strive for excellence, NEVER perfection.** Your goal should be to work hard and get better. Understand that perfect is the enemy of great. Don't get overly frustrated when results from your efforts aren't immediate. Don't dwell on disappointment; learn from it. And don't compare yourself to others. Your growth as an athlete is all that matters and all you can control.

3. **Identify a support team and use them.** Who can you talk to about sport-related frustrations? Who can you talk to about school concerns? Friend issues? When you're sad? Have answers to these questions and get comfortable utilizing these valuable resources.

4. **Create some balance in your life.** Maintain some relationships that extend beyond your teammates. Cultivate your nonsport interests and talents. If you enjoy more than one sport, don't feel pressured to specialize or play year-round.

5. **Know the symptoms of burnout.** If identified early, burnout is easy to address—just take a break, step back, talk to someone. If ignored, burnout can create a love-hate relationship between athletes and their sport or, worse, chase them out of it. Symptoms of sports burnout include decreased pleasure from participation, vague injuries or frequent illness, excess tension, increased emotional and physical fatigue, irritability, and sleep difficulties.

Training Note: Helpful with the following Mental Mechanics: Confidence, Mindset, Emotions, Resilience, Drive

WORKSHEET #15

· · · · ·

PLAY GROUNDED

YOUR SPORTS CREDO

How do you think about your sport? How do you think about yourself as a player of that sport? Do you have a set of beliefs and principles that help guide your actions and reactions when you train and play? In other words, do you have a sports credo?

Being grounded in a realistic and positive philosophy with respect to your sport and yourself as a competitive athlete can help you before, during, and after competing. It can keep you from slipping into the unrealistic expectations and harsh judgments that have a negative impact on performance and steal the joy from the game you love. Anchoring yourself to a sports credo that respects both the game and yourself and will help you play grounded.

A good way to develop your *Sports Credo* is to become very clear about how you think about your sport and how you want to play it. Finish the statements below and use them to identify the beliefs and principles that will help guide you throughout your athletic journey.

PLAYING GROUNDED
SPORTS CREDO WORKSHEET
GROUNDING STATEMENTS:

- I love my sport because...

- Things that make my sport challenging (and sometimes frustrating) are...

- The way I want to handle these challenges is...

- I play my best when...

- I show respect for my sport and myself by...

- After a game/match I want to be able to say...

SAMPLE SPORTS CREDO:

I love my sport because it's exciting, challenging, and fun. I pursue excellence in my sport, not perfection. I know that I play my best when I trust my game, play with passion, and look like I'm having fun. I also know that thinking too much and judging myself never helps and takes the fun out of the game. I believe that I will have a great game every game and accept the reality that NO athlete plays great every time. I view challenges and setbacks as opportunities to get better and grow as an athlete. When the game is over, I want to be able to say I gave 100 percent, played my game, and had a blast.

MY SPORTS CREDO:

Training Note: Helpful with the following Mental Mechanics: Confidence, Mindset, Emotion, Resilience, Drive

POSTSCRIPT

· · · · ·

TO PARENTS AND COACHES

If you are the parent or coach of a young athlete, you know how rewarding your experience can be. I was also a sports parent and coach, and I love nothing more than watching my kids play and sharing that experience with them. But let's face it: it's easy to get caught up in the competition. I know there have been times when I've been too loud or too excited or said things that put undue pressure on my children. I've stepped in it royally. Maybe you have, too. If so, welcome to the club.

The good news is that we can work on our mental games, too. I hope this book serves your athlete well, but I also hope it will help you realize the importance of the mental game for all of us. We know our kids better than anyone. We see things that even they may not yet understand themselves. If we work on our mental games—how we think, what we say, and what we do—we can be an asset to our kids so they can be free to just play.

IT'S ALL ABOUT THE BALANCE

The mental game can be understood and worked on. It's not a vague concept. It's a tool that can be developed, trained, and mastered—just like the technical and physical aspects of a sport.

Neglecting the mental gear can cause an imbalance in your athlete that can lead to burnout and frustration. However, when you treat the mental gear with the same respect and importance as the technical and physical gears, balance is established, and your athlete's hard work will pay bigger dividends.

An underdeveloped mental gear negatively affects performance, but it can also take away the pleasure athletes get from participating in their sport. Strengthening the mental gear adds a vital dimension to an athlete's game that can be seen in their play and on their faces. They may even have an edge over their opponents!

Understanding the mental game can also be the great equalizer. It means kids with strong mental mechanics who may not be the biggest or most gifted athletes on the field can find a way to get the job done.

TALK THE TALK

Our children follow our lead, and we can take an active role in helping them become complete athletes. If we take the mental game seriously, they will, too. If you want to give your athletes the tools to handle the pressures of the game, it can be as easy as knowing how to talk to them. Talk to them about things they can control, like effort and attitude. Let your encouragement help them learn to focus on process ("Be aggressive at the plate") rather than outcome ("Get a hit"). If you talk about mental mechanics as a strength and encourage your athlete to make the connection between how they think and how they play, they will be motivated to work on this aspect of their game.

I want parents and coaches to feel empowered to discuss the mental game and offer specific ways to help their athletes grow and improve. Help them with their thinking when you recognize it's not benefiting their game. Instead of saying, "You have to be mentally tough," or "Don't let it bother you"—both of which are vague and provide no direction—you can discuss resilience or tools to help manage emotions. If you avoid clichés and focus on *process* over *outcome*, you will help direct your athlete's mindset toward fixing something they have control over, rather than dwelling on something that's in the past.

Be aware that what you say may be inadvertently putting unnecessary pressure on your kids. Remember, athletes are playing a *game*. Starting with "Did you have fun?" sets a better tone than "Did you win?" and maintains a healthy perspective. Of course, you want to talk about the game and how your athlete played. My suggestion is simply to keep the conversation balanced. Otherwise, you end up with an athlete who believes *Dad's only happy when we win*, or *I have to score for Mom to think I played well*.

The "fun" question is also important for another reason. If your athlete isn't having fun, they're not in the BOX. Help your athlete recognize that not having fun is an indication that their mental mechanics need to be tweaked. Don't let them view having fun as a reward for playing well but, rather, as a key ingredient that helps them to play well. We all play better when we're having fun!

Simply noticing examples of good mental mechanics as a parent or a coach and sharing them with your athlete can facilitate the development of the athlete's mental game. Commenting on process—things they *do*—such as "I love how you were aggressive on defense today," or "You did a great job of shooting without hesitating," will help them to also emphasize process over outcome.

By complimenting specific mental mechanics—saying, for example, "I was really proud of your resilience after that turnover," or "I thought you had a great mindset the entire game"—will encourage your athlete to value the mental gear and motivate them to continue working on it.

ATTITUDE IS EVERYTHING

Remember: it's not a sign of weakness if your athlete needs to work on their mental gear. *Every athlete* needs to work on their mental gear! Some great athletes may seem innately confident and focused, but they also have to work on their mental game. Everyone should. Parents and coaches can help their athlete by setting the appropriate attitude toward the mental gear. It's not something to be embarrassed about or spoken about in hushed tones.

Instead, reinforce to your athlete that the mental gear is just as important as the other two gears. It's part of the balance that unlocks potential and makes playing fun. A complete athlete is born with the equipment she needs, and one component of that equipment is the brain. It makes sense to train your brain just like you train your muscles and practice your skills. The brain is the command center for every one of those muscles and the skills they execute.

Encourage your athlete to use this book to become a complete and balanced athlete. Frame it as a training guide for athletes who want to reach their full potential and thrive in their sport, not as a self-help book for athletes who struggle.

You are the expert on your kids. If you see that your athlete needs coaching on a mental mechanic, encourage them to do the exercises and worksheets in Chapter 7. If it feels like homework, or if your athlete is perfectly happy playing at their current level, let them be happy. Let it be fun!

A FINAL NOTE

We love our children. They love sports. We are their biggest fans. Obviously, we want the best for our athletes, and our intentions are usually in the right place. Sometimes, however, our passion gets in our way, and a throwaway comment to the athlete can undo a lot of good work.

A father of one of my athletes loved his son very much and wanted to do everything he could to build the young wrestler's confidence. He wanted him to believe in his own greatness, so every time they went to a meet, the dad would tell him, "You are the best wrestler out there. You are the best wrestler in the state."

But he wasn't. He was very good, but he wasn't the best

wrestler in the state. The son knew how he performed and started to fear he'd never measure up to his father's expectations. The son worried that he was constantly disappointing his dad. Imagine the relief the wrestler felt when his dad shifted to process-oriented statements: "Just go out and do your job. You're so quick and explosive. Use your strengths." Then the wrestler had something to work with. He knew exactly what to do. He didn't let the BOX get cluttered with worries about outcomes and expectations. He just relaxed and wrestled. Not surprisingly, his performance improved. His dad said they both found meets a lot more enjoyable.

As parents and coaches, we all have a big influence on how our athletes think and feel about their game and themselves. They pay very close attention to us. What we say and what we do has an impact. By focusing on the mental game—our athlete's and our own—we can see to it that the impact is positive and contributes to the development of a complete athlete. An athlete who is happy and playing their best.

ABOUT THE AUTHOR

DR. PETE TEMPLE, the founder and president of Mind's Eye Sports Performance in Geneva, Illinois, has worked as a clinical and performance psychologist for over twenty years. He works with athletes at all levels, from middle school to the professional ranks, helping them develop strong mental games for sports and life. He is also an advisor for The Right Profile, which assesses athletes for a wide variety of professional sports teams. He has a bachelor's degree from DePauw University and a doctorate, with honors, from the Chicago School of Professional Psychology. A three-sport athlete and former college quarterback, he is a member of his high school Hall of Fame. Dr. Temple is married with two adult children.

Made in the USA
Coppell, TX
13 May 2021